FAST FABULOUS
DESSERTS

March 23, 1985

to Maryanne:

Best regards & Hope
you like the book.

Love & Kisses

Jack Lirio

by the same author

COOKING WITH JACK LIRIO

JACK LIRIO

FAST FABULOUS DESSERTS

E. P. DUTTON, INC.   NEW YORK

Published in the United States by E.P. Dutton, Inc.
2 Park Avenue, New York, N.Y. 10016

Library of Congress Cataloging in Publication Data
Lirio, Jack.
Fast fabulous desserts.
Includes index.
1. Desserts. I. Title.
TX773.L495   1984   641.8′6   84-10188
ISBN 0-525-24275-9

Published simultaneously in Canada by Fitzhenry & Whiteside Limited,
Toronto

DESIGNED BY EARL TIDWELL

10 9 8 7 6 5 4 3 2 1
COBE
First Edition

TO JERRY MARCH,
TESTER, TASTER, AND FRIEND

CONTENTS

Acknowledgments
ix

Introduction
1

A Note on Ingredients
7

Equipment and Procedures
10

1   Fresh Fruit Desserts
23

2   Cooked Fruit Desserts
49

3   Baked Custards and Puddings
73

4   Creams and Mousses
89

5   Pies, Tarts, and Cheesecakes
111

6   Cakes, Simple and Fancy
145

7   Entertaining Trifles
177

8   Spectacular Cake Desserts
199

9   Spectacular Light Cake Desserts
223

10   Ice Creams and Frozen Desserts
251

Index
283

I should like to thank my editor, Diane Harris, for her guidance and help, and for being the nicest, most diplomatic editor in the whole world. Diane is leaving to start a new career. I wish her well, but will miss her terribly.

Thanks to my colleagues in the business in San Francisco from whom I have learned a great deal: Diane Dexter, Jim Dodge, Alice Medrich, and Donna Nordin. And thanks to Mary Risley for giving them a place to teach. *Merci, Tante Marie.*

FAST FABULOUS DESSERTS

INTRODUCTION

The desserts in this book are quick to prepare, beautiful—
often spectacular—in appearance, and incredibly good-tasting. That is why they are called fast and fabulous. Make
them with top-quality fruits, berries, nuts, and other ingredients and even the simplest will be truly fabulous, as
the title promises. We may have a little more trouble agree-
ing on the word *fast.*

Many of these desserts are fast in anybody's under-
standing of the word. A fair number of them can be done
in only 15 to 20 minutes' total time. Others are equally
quick to prepare, but require some do-ahead time for baking
and cooling, jelling, or freezing.

The vast majority of desserts in this book can be prepared in less than an hour. A few of the more elaborate ones
may take longer, but the nice thing about them is that they
can be done ahead and can be prepared in short segments
of work. You will find doing them quite painless and really

1

fun; and little or none of your valuable time will be required on the day of the dinner or special occasion.

Almost every dessert and pastry technique that exists has been simplified in this book. I have experimented with every imaginable shortcut and labor-saving trick to produce recipes that are streamlined to the ultimate degree. In some cases, to save time, prepared commercial products have been used, but these have been strictly quality products. This was a new field for me and I was amazed at how many wholesome prepared products I was able to find: ice creams and ices, cookies, chocolates, canned and frozen fruits, fruit sauces, and so on. According to the labels on these products, they contain strictly home-quality ingredients, are free of those multisyllabic chemical preservatives, and of mysterious initialed ones, and are free also of artificial flavorings and colors.

For those of you who have more time to spend and who may think I have gone too far in my use of prepared products, you are free to poach your own pears instead of using canned; you may make your own brownies instead of using Sara Lee's, and make your own ice creams instead of buying them. Your desserts may not be fast as mine, but they are apt to be be even more fabulous.

As I mentioned above, the quality of the raw materials used in your desserts plays an important role in how fabulous they will be. However, in addition to this critical element, there are some other important considerations that influence how successful a certain dessert will be. One of these is the suitability of a dessert in a certain menu. What is fabulous on one occasion may seem overdone on another. What is light and perfect at the end of a heavy meal may seem too unadorned after a simply prepared lunch or supper. There is also the question of timing: The first perfectly ripe local strawberries of the season can be fabulous all by themselves, whereas three weeks later, they may require a slightly more elaborate treatment to create the same excitement.

For those of you working on overloaded schedules, I thought it might be useful to provide a rundown of the four categories of fast that are to be found in the book and some of the desserts that belong in them.

VERY FAST — 15 TO 20 MINUTES

These very fast desserts are virtually instant desserts; quick assembly jobs requiring little more than a quick wash, a slice, and perhaps a fast whipping of some cream. Each has its little feature or twist that gives it that fabulous touch. Here are some desserts from the book that fall into this category:

PEACHES WITH BLUEBERRIES IN RASPBERRY CREAM

PEARS WITH CRANBERRY-ORANGE SAUCE

PINEAPPLE WITH COCONUT, BROWN SUGAR, AND RUM

PURPLE PLUMS CHANTILLY

STRAWBERRIES AND KIWIS IN COINTREAU FROZEN CREAM

SPICED APPLE BROWNIE TRIFLE

PINEAPPLE ANGEL FOOD TRIFLE

MAPLE PECAN COUPE

RASPBERRY COUPE WITH GRAND MARNIER

FLEUR-DE-LYS

FAST, BUT MUST BE STARTED
AHEAD — 15 TO 20 MINUTES

This category includes dishes that actually take only 15 to 20 minutes of working time, but that require time to bake or cook, and to cool; to jell, or to freeze, and so on. Here are some desserts in this category:

BLUEBERRIES AND BANANAS WITH ENGLISH CREAM

SLICED PEACHES IN BLACKBERRY SAUCE

PEARS WITH SOFT-FROZEN STRAWBERRY SAUCE

WORLD'S BEST BLACK CHERRY COMPOTE

PEACHES IN SPICED RED WINE

GROUND ALMOND CAKE

CHOCOLATE SAUCE CAKE

BLUEBERRY COUPE

COFFEE CHOCOLATE COUPE

PECAN BALLS WITH BROWN SUGAR SAUCE

MODERATELY FAST — 30 TO 60 MINUTES

The best thing about the dishes in this category is that they can be done days or weeks ahead, and in stages, as already mentioned. Here are some of the many desserts that fall into this group:

STRAWBERRY-RASPBERRY CUSTARD

LIME MOUSSE WITH CANDIED PEEL

CHOCOLATE PIE, WALNUT CHOCOLATE CRUST

NO-BAKE LEMON CHEESECAKE

BLACKBERRY KUCHEN

CHOCOLATE BABA CAKE

BAVARIAN CREAM TRIFLE WITH STRAWBERRIES

CHOCOLATE-COATED PEAR CAKE

TOASTED HAZELNUT COUPE

FROZEN CHOCOLATE SQUARES

FAST CONSIDERING COMPLEXITY OF DISH — 1 TO 2 HOURS

Only the recipes in Chapters 8 and 9 fall into this category. They are the spectacular cake desserts, and the spectacular light cake desserts. Most of these are so elaborate and so beautiful that your guests will think that instead of an hour and a half, you spent all day on them. Prepare these desserts in stages and you will be amazed at how little time they take.

A nice bonus to the desserts in Chapter 9 is that the base spongecake recipes yield an extra cake to be frozen and used for a future dessert. That means that your second spectacular dessert will take only 30 to 60 minutes. Here are some of the desserts from Chapters 8 and 9:

ALMOND MOCHA TORTE

CHERRY DOME CAKE

CHOCOLATE CREAM CAKE

CHOCOLATE MOUSSE CAKE WITH STRAWBERRIES

WALNUT TORTE WITH PEACHES AND CREAM

PINEAPPLE-COCONUT CAKE-TART

RASPBERRY-APPLESAUCE CAKE-TART
CARAMEL PECAN SURPRISE CAKE
LIME MERINGUE CAKE
STRAWBERRY TAJ MAHAL

A NOTE ON INGREDIENTS

When I was a kid growing up in southern New Jersey, my father used to drive five miles out of town in the summer to buy cantaloupes. And he would buy them from only one particular farmer. Other farmers would get his business for other things—for peaches, for corn, for lima beans, and for apples. From living in the area for a long time, Dad had learned exactly which farmer grew the very best of each kind of fruit or vegetable. The farmer who sold us our corn won out because he would go into the fields and pick the ears while we waited. In cities today, or in small towns, you must do the equivalent of what my father used to do. You must ferret out the best sources of fruits and vegetables if you are to serve fabulous food.

Of course, there are a lot of dishes here that don't depend upon fresh fruits in season. The book contains lots of midwinter desserts you can make from frozen raspberries, canned blueberries, cherries, and pineapple; chocolate; rum and orange liqueur; walnuts, pecans, and raisins. These desserts can be just as delectable, although perhaps in a different way. And good ingredients matter here too. Search out the best in every category.

DESSERTS AND NUTRITION

How do these desserts fit into our new guidelines for good nutrition? The desserts in this book contain wonderfully nutritious things such as fruit, fruit juice, milk, eggs, nuts, seeds, white and whole-wheat flours, rice, oats, butter, oil —elements, in short, that are the very core of good nutrition in the human diet. There are many people who live their whole lives on nothing but these things plus vegetables and they are healthy and perhaps live longer than the rest of us. Of course, desserts practically all call for sugar, and sugar is bad for you, isn't it?

Obviously too much of it is, but it appears that moderate amounts are not hazardous for the average person. There is a great deal still not known about sugar. So far, at least, nothing specific has been proved linking it to heart disease or to cancer, but there is a feeling among most people that consuming large amounts of sugar daily is not good. The problem is not eating desserts once or twice a week but rather daily habits of eating and drinking large quantities of soft drinks, sugared coffee, ice cream, cookies, packaged cakes, candy bars, and the like.

Also, why do I use butter instead of margarine?

I prefer the taste of butter. Also, because butter has been used in Europe for cakes, pastries, and desserts for centuries, it is an established tradition. Things don't taste "right" without it. Aside from that, from the cholesterol standpoint, I believe that margarine, particularly hard margarine, may be worse for our bodies than butter. There is evidence that appears to indicate that, in addition to saturated-fat-related heart problems, "partially hydrogenated" margarine may also be a factor in colon and breast cancers. It appears that we need to cut down generally on all fats in our daily lives, but I think that the human body can tolerate the fat involved in an occasional dessert treat, regardless of which one it is. Choose the one you like best.

EQUIPMENT AND PROCEDURES

BEATING EGG YOLKS

Try not to overbeat egg yolks. For spongecakes particularly, some experienced bakers don't beat the yolks at all but just stir them to mix, then fold them into the beaten whites. I frankly prefer the results I get from beating the yolks, but I mention this so that you will realize that underbeating is much preferred to overbeating.

BEATING EGG WHITES

This is one of the most critical elements in cake baking. People in general tend to overbeat egg whites. I think it's because they are afraid they haven't beaten them enough. For cakes in general, it is better to underbeat egg whites rather than to overbeat. Fortunately, there is a good test for letting you know just the right moment in beating egg whites. It is called the *inverted bowl test.* When you can turn the bowl upside down and the beaten whites do not fall out, they are ready to use in cake making. I suggest you invert the bowl carefully at first. Should the egg whites fall onto the floor during the test, it can be difficult getting them back into the bowl.

Here is something else about the inverted bowl test: If you are using a hand-held electric mixer, you must swirl the beaters to get all the mixture into the action; otherwise, the part clinging to the sides of the bowl may not get beaten enough to hold on. Swirl the beaters as you beat, moving them around and up and down near the edge of the bowl, bringing them as close to the bowl as you can without actually hitting it. Striking a bowl, particularly a metal bowl, with metal mixer blades causes microscopic metal chips to fly into the egg whites, a prospect that does not appeal to me in the least.

GRATING ORANGE OR LEMON ZEST

The zest of an orange is the orange part of the outer skin. Scraped or grated from the orange and added to cakes and desserts, it gives a special flavor that is obtained in no other way. Lemon and lime zest are also used this same way. The trick in obtaining the zest is to get only the colored part of the skin and not the bitter white part that is just underneath.

To remove the zest, you may use a fine grater or a

vegetable peeler (chopping the peel afterward with a knife), but I find the fastest, neatest method is to use a small tool called a *zesteur*. This is a wood-handled tool with a metal fitting containing a row of 5 small holes. You scrape this metal piece across the orange, lemon, or lime, and it gives you long, skinny strips of zest. You can either chop these strips fine with a knife, or you can put them in a food processor fitted with the steel blade, adding sugar to be used in the recipe, and process until the zest is ground fine.

CHOPPING NUTS

The recipes in this book often call for nuts to be chopped in $\frac{1}{4}$-inch dice or in $\frac{1}{8}$-inch dice. Does that mean that you must take each nut piece and chop it into exactly that size?

No, it certainly doesn't. It would be nice if you could, but not very practical. Instructions to chop in $\frac{1}{4}$-inch or $\frac{1}{8}$-inch dice are meant to give you a guideline of how large the average nut piece should be. To chop in $\frac{1}{4}$-inch dice, for example, simply chop the nuts, either on a board using a large, sharp knife or in the food processor using the steel blade. In either case, when half of the nuts are approximately the size you want, with a quarter of them being larger and another quarter smaller, stop. You are there.

FOOD PROCESSORS

First, let me say that there are plenty of recipes in the book that don't require a food processor. But any cook who is pressed for time will bless the day he or she buys one. For those who don't have a processor, depending upon the recipe, you might use an electric mixer, a pastry blender, a food mill, a nut grinder, or simply two sharp knives. The big thing about a food processor is that it saves you time and generally does the job better. It has simplified a lot of complicated dishes that used to be done only in restaurants or in kitchens where they had lots of servants. The processor will open up a range of new dishes for you. Get one. Ask for one for Christmas or for your next birthday.

IF YOU DO NOT HAVE A MICROWAVE OVEN

You will find the microwave oven used in some of the recipes in this book. For those of you who may not have one, here are some alternate ways of doing the two main jobs calling for it.

When melting chocolate, instead of using the microwave, you may simply melt the chocolate in a double boiler. Make sure that the water in the bottom container is hot, but not boiling; be especially careful not to splash even the slightest amount of water in the chocolate.

When heating gelatin with small amounts of liquid, the best alternate method is to place the gelatin mixture in a tiny saucepan or a metal measuring cup; then put the cup in a pan containing an inch of boiling water. Heat the gelatin plus liquid, stirring occasionally, until it is hot and the gelatin has dissolved.

PIPING WHIPPED CREAM FOR DECORATIONS

Many of the recipes in this book call for piping whipped-cream decorations on the tops of fruit desserts, cakes, pies, and so on. Generally this simply means to whip a cup of cream, and stir in in 2 tablespoons of powdered sugar plus a teaspoon of vanilla and/or a tablespoon or two of a sweet liqueur (Grand Marnier, Cointreau, Amaretto, apricot liqueur). To do it the easy way, simply spoon this cream over the desserts and serve.

There is a fancier way, however, a way that will make your desserts look considerably more fabulous. Pipe the cream using a pastry bag and tip. The bags and tips are available in kitchen shops. I suggest buying a plastic-lined bag 14 or 16 inches long. The tips are reasonable, so buy a small assortment. Get the "open star" series in several different sizes (Ateco 0, 3, 6, 8). There is also an interesting pastry series I like that has more points sticking up and is a little more ornate (Ateco 0-B, 3-B, 6-B, 8-B). Having these eight tips will give you many options when piping decorations.

To do the actual piping, fill the bag, then hold it straight up in the air with the tip close (¼ inch) to what you are piping onto. Squeeze, raising the tip slightly as the decoration appears. Stop squeezing and pull away. That's all there is to it. There is another decoration you might try that calls for swirling a small circle instead of squeezing a stationary pouf. Try one of these on your counter top, and if it works, do it on the dessert. If your decorations do not look sharp and well defined, whip the cream a little stiffer. For additional ideas for decorating pies with whipped cream, see the introduction to Chapter 5.

HINTS FOR NO-FAIL CAKE MAKING

These hints and suggestions are meant to give further information and assistance in making and handling the cakes in this book. They apply especially to the three Butter Spongecake Layers in Chapter 9. The procedures in the recipes themselves are already simplified and no-fail, I believe, but further details about the following steps in cake making should be helpful.

PREPARING CAKE TINS

One of life's darkest moments is having a baked cake stick to the bottom of the tin when you try to unmold it. To avoid this, some people put a parchment paper circle in the bottom of each cake pan. I prefer to butter and flour the tins very well, generally using cold butter (as I have forgotten to take it out of the refrigerator earlier), slicing off two or three thin pieces for each tin, then smearing the butter down with my thumb to soften it, and finally rubbing a good coating all over the bottom and sides of the tin.

To flour a cake tin after buttering it, put 1 or 2 tablespoons of flour into the tin and tilt and turn so that the flour sticks to the butter all over the bottom and sides of the tin. Drop the tin, letting it bang on the counter, then turn it over and dump any excess flour into the second tin. Then flour the second tin the same way.

With springform tins there is a problem. If you butter them with the lavish amount of butter described above, the butter melts in the oven, runs out the crack in the bottom of the tin, burns on the bottom of the oven, and smells up the kitchen. So, for springform cakes, use 1 or 2 teaspoons only of melted butter per tin, rubbing it over the bottom and sides of the tin with your fingers. Finish by flouring in the normal way.

POSITION OF CAKES IN THE OVEN

When baking two cakes in one relatively small home oven, I find that placing one cake directly under the other cake in the center of the oven gives the best results. The cakes will bake evenly, although you may have to bake the bottom cake an extra 5 minutes or so. Try to arrange the oven shelves so that there is a reasonable amount of space between the two cakes, but don't let the lower cake get too close to the bottom of the oven.

MEASURING FLOUR

In some parts of the country, particularly in warm, damp climates, it is advisable to sift flour several times when making cakes. The dampness gets into the flour and makes it clump, causing confusion in measuring and also causing tiny flour lumps to appear in the cakes after baking. In the area where I live, which is generally cool and not too wet, I get away with very little sifting. I measure flour by fluffing it into a cup using a spoon or scoop, then scraping the cup level with a knife. The flour is then mixed with other dry ingredients in the recipe such as cocoa or baking powder, and loaded into a sifter to be sifted later onto the eggs.

When cutting a cake into layers, if you should see tiny little balls of flour that have not combined with the batter, ignore them for the time being, but in the future, sift the flour two or three times before using.

BOWL SIZES

Bowl sizes are critical in cake making. If you place 8 egg yolks, ¾ cup sugar, and a very small amount of lemon juice in a *huge* bowl you will find that you have only about a ½-inch-deep puddle of mixture. In trying to beat this with a hand-held electric mixer, the beaters will hardly go down into the mass at all and beating will be very inefficient. If you place these same ingredients, however, in a 4-cup bowl, particularly if the bowl is high and rounded, the mass will come up at least twice as high and when the mixer is turned on, the beaters will be submerged in the batter and the machine can do its work.

For the Basic Spongecake Layers, try to use a 4-cup bowl for the yolks and a 6-cup bowl for the whites. Have a good, large mixing bowl for gathering all the batter at the end.

ELECTRIC MIXERS

An inexpensive hand-held electric mixer is the perfect thing to use for any recipe in this book calling for a mixer. In all the recipes in this book, I have used only my small, inexpensive, hand-held Sunbeam Mixmaster. I almost always beat at high speed, pushing the little button in the handle for an extra "burst of power," and away I go.

If you happen to have a powerful electric mixer on a stand, such as a Kitchen Aid or Kenwood, I recommend beating yolks or whites in it at just past its medium speed (#6 out of 10 speeds on the Kitchen Aid). When beating egg whites, start checking about halfway through the times suggested in the recipes.

INTERRUPTIONS

There is a 10- to 15-minute period in cake making when you should not allow yourself to be interrupted by anything short of the house catching on fire. It starts with that moment when you are all done with the preliminary steps. You have the oven on, the cake tins buttered and floured, the dry ingredients measured and in the sifter, the eggs separated, the butter melted, and the lemons zested and squeezed. You are now ready to start working with the eggs.

Take the phone off the hook; put the baby to bed; lower the shades; disconnect the doorbell; put on sunglasses; insert earplugs; abandon all connection with the outside world. For 10 to 12 minutes, just concentrate on the cake. It's even good to memorize the few remaining operations so that you can perform them without having to take time to stop and read the recipe. From the time you start beating the yolks to that moment when the cakes go into the oven, do your level best to avoid even the slightest interruption. I think this is one of the most important elements in no-fail cake making.

WHEN IS A CAKE DONE?

In 30 years of cake baking, I am still not always sure when cakes are done. Here are some of the things I suggest plus a few of the thoughts that go through my head as I'm testing cakes for doneness.

1. In white or yellow cakes, look for nice brown color on the tops of the cakes before even trying any other tests.

2. When a cake has pulled away from the sides of the tin, you can be pretty sure it's done. Certain nut tortes,

however, can pull away quite a bit and still not be done.

3. I generally like the "feel" test. This is not very specific and depends somewhat upon experience. Generally, if you touch a cake and your hand disappears into the batter, the cake is not done. Seriously, however, when a cake feels firm as opposed to soft and gooey, it indicates that it is done. This touch test is not a good one for spongecakes, which are so soft that they still don't feel done to me when they actually are.

4. I don't generally like the toothpick test, although I sometimes use it. In the past I have poked cakes with toothpicks and have seem them come out impeccably clean, only to find out later that the cakes were not done.

5. Some cakes may be deliberately underbaked in the center and still be marvelous, so don't jump off a cliff if your cake is not quite done. The major problem for these cakes is that they sink and it takes a bit of doing to make them look beautiful.

6. I worry about overbaking as it can cause cakes to become dry. However, if a cake has a fair amount of butter in it (4 ounces of butter to 1 or 1½ cups flour), it is not so critical, as the fat helps keep the cake moist even if it is slightly overbaked.

ON OPENING THE OVEN DOOR
TO SEE IF A CAKE IS DONE

There is an art to this. It involves really fast peeks, keen powers of observation, split-second decision making, and getting the oven door closed in a hurry so that the oven does not cool off. Here is a good chronological peeking order for baked-cake testing:

PEEK #1. This is a one-second preliminary peek, mainly out of obligation, as the cake really has 5 more minutes to go and you're pretty sure it isn't done. In one second, all you think about is if the cake is brown. If it's not, give it 5 or 10 more minutes.

PEEK #2. This is another one-second peek, but this time you feel that the cake really might be done. Look for brown color and/or shrinking from the sides of the tin, if you can do both things in one second. If not, you may give two one-second peeks.

PEEK #3. This one is known as the quick feel. It is a two-second peek and a follow-up one. The cake looked brown the last time you looked and it appeared to have shrunk away from the sides. You are checking again for further assurance that the cake is done. Open the oven door. Poke your hand in very fast and push down on the center of the cake. Quickly pull back and close the oven door instantly. Carefully consider now what you felt and decide if the cake is done or not.

PEEK #4. Now you're getting serious. Five or 10 minutes have gone by since the last peek. Things were already almost there, so it is undoubtedly really done now. Have a pot holder handy, then open the oven door; grab the cake fast; pull it out of the oven, and close the door immediately! Take time now to feel further or poke with a toothpick, but decide quickly. If the cake is not done, you must get it back into the oven in a hurry.

CAKE RACKS AND UNMOLDING CAKES

It is handy, but not necessary, in cake making to have some cake racks. These are round, low, wire racks about 12 inches in diameter that are perfect to use for unmolding and cooling cakes. For cakes that need to be unmolded right out of the oven while they are still hot, such as the Butter

Spongecake Layers in Chapter 8, it is advisable to have three racks for two cakes, as I will explain.

Butter Spongecake Layers are specified to be baked in springform tins. As soon as they are done, they should be removed from the oven and unmolded. First cut around the sides of the cakes with a small knife to make sure the cakes are not stuck to the tins. Next open the springform clasp and remove the side of the tin. Some people do this by setting the cake on a can of tomatoes. (It can be chicken soup if you prefer.) Loosen the springform clasp and let the sides fall down for easy removal.

Next place a cake rack on top of the cake and invert the cake onto the rack. Cut to loosen and remove the bottom of the cake tin, then place another rack on top of the cake and flip the whole thing over so that the cake is right side up again. Perform the same operation on the second cake. You will notice that it takes two racks to flip over the second cake, which is why it takes three racks to unmold two cakes.

CUTTING CAKES INTO LAYERS

This can be traumatic, but it shouldn't be. Here is any easy way to cut a cake into two or three layers. Cut around the side of the cake with a sharp knife, cutting into the cake just the width of the knife. It is as if you were cutting guidelines. Either cut one ring with a knife, as if you were cutting the cake in half, or cut two rings as if to cut the cake into thirds. Get your eyes down there so you can see what you're doing. Once the rings are cut, bury a length of regular sewing thread in one of the rings you have cut. Cross the thread over in an X where the two ends meet, then pull straight out; not up or down, but out. As you pull, the thread will cut the cake into even layers. If you have cut two rings, bury the thread again in the second ring and repeat the procedure.

FREEZING OR REFRIGERATING CAKES

If not using cake layers right away, do not keep them in the refrigerator, but wrap them well in plastic (I use refrigerator-weight plastic bags) and freeze them as soon as they are baked and cooled. This will keep them at their freshest and best. As soon as cakes or pastries containing perishable whipped-cream fillings are assembled, they must be refrigerated, but avoid assembling them more than one or two days ahead, as refrigeration seems to dry out baked goods.

1

FRESH FRUIT DESSERTS

BLUEBERRIES AND BANANAS WITH ENGLISH CREAM

GRAPES IN RUM BUTTERSCOTCH CREAM

GRAPES IN SHERRIED CREAM

MIXED FRUIT IN CANTALOUPE RINGS

SLICED PEACHES IN BLACKBERRY SAUCE

PEACHES WITH BLUEBERRIES IN RASPBERRY CREAM

PEACHES WITH GRAND MARNIER WHIPPED CREAM

PEARS WITH CRANBERRY-ORANGE SAUCE

PEARS WITH SOFT-FROZEN STRAWBERRY SAUCE

PINEAPPLE WITH CARROT-LIME CREAM

PINEAPPLE WITH COCONUT, BROWN SUGAR, AND RUM

PURPLE PLUMS CHANTILLY

STRAWBERRIES WITH CHOCOLATE CREAM AND CHOCOLATE SAUCE

STRAWBERRIES AND KIWIS IN COINTREAU FROZEN CREAM

STRAWBERRIES IN STRAWBERRY SOUR CREAM

Fresh fruits in their seasons, what a glorious gift to man! Beautiful ripe peaches, a honey-sweet melon, a bowlful of fragrant, red, flavorful strawberries! When you start with these wonderful things, your job in the kitchen is an easy one. Combining perfectly ripe strawberries with cream or sour cream is a matter of minutes. Blueberries also inspire a variety of quick-to-make delights. And think of ripe peaches! Or try pineapple with a sauce of coconut and rum. First, always search out fruit at its peak. Then present it in the simple ways suggested here and you will be serving the prettiest, quickest, most delicious desserts that exist.

To find wonderful fruit generally means you must respect the seasons. Learn when fruits are at their best in your area and find the best nearby markets. Don't be satisfied unless the fruit is really good. It's a mistake to serve fruit desserts that aren't superlative. If you can't find good fruit, turn to another chapter and look for something else to serve. Make a pudding or a cake or do something with ice cream. I am convinced that if we stopped buying so much poor-quality fruit, farmers would give us better stuff.

The fruits featured in this chapter are essentially spring and summer fruits, those that can be sliced and served as desserts, as is. You will find the winter fruits in a variety of cooked desserts in chapters ahead.

Here are some of my favorite desserts in this chapter, listed alphabetically rather than in order of preference, because I couldn't make up my mind: Pears with Cranberry-Orange Sauce, Pineapple with Carrot-Lime Cream, Purple Plums Chantilly, Strawberries with Chocolate Cream and Chocolate Sauce, and Strawberries and Kiwis in Cointreau Frozen Cream.

BLUEBERRIES AND BANANAS
WITH ENGLISH CREAM
(serves 6)

This is a delightful dessert to serve in the summer when fresh blueberries are in season. If you should find some especially nice, inexpensive ones, you might buy 2 or 3 pints and leave out the bananas. Either way, it's a wonderful dessert.

INGREDIENTS:

2 cups milk
6 egg yolks
½ cup + 2 tablespoons
    sugar (total)
2 teaspoons vanilla

2 tablespoons orange
    liqueur (optional)
1 pint blueberries
6 ripe bananas

SERVING DISHES: 6 individual dessert saucers

PROCEDURE:

1. First make the English Cream. Have ready on the side ½ cup cold milk, a clean bowl, and a rubber spatula.

2. Place 1½ cups milk, yolks, and ½ cup sugar in a saucepan (preferably heavy). Over medium-high heat, whisking occasionally, bring just to the *first signs* of a boil (about 4 minutes).

3. Immediately whisk in the reserved ½ cup cold milk, then pour the mixture into a clean bowl. With a rubber spatula, scrape any curdled part from the bottom of the pan, adding it to the mixture.

4. Add vanilla plus (optional) orange liqueur and stir to mix. Refrigerate uncovered until chilled, then cover with plastic.

5. Inspect blueberries, discarding stems and leaves. Wash (if you think necessary) and dry well. Sprinkle 2 tablespoons sugar over berries, then stir and reserve in refrigerator until serving time.

TO SERVE: Slice bananas into serving dishes. Add blueberries, then spoon English Cream on top. Serve.

DO-AHEAD INFORMATION: The English Cream may be prepared 1 or 2 days ahead or frozen for 1 or 2 weeks.

CAUTION: Keep refrigerated and do not keep longer than suggested times, as it is very perishable even chilled or frozen. The blueberries may be prepared a day ahead, but the bananas must be sliced at the last minute or they will darken.

GRAPES IN RUM BUTTERSCOTCH CREAM
(serves 6)

The secret of success in this wonderful dessert is in finding good grapes. Thompson seedless can be sweet and wonderful if they are ripe, but unpleasant and acid if they are not. Ribier and other grapes with seeds can be excellent in this dessert, but they require a little more work, as they need to be cut in half and the seeds removed.

INGREDIENTS:

¾ cup (packed) dark brown sugar

¼ cup water

3 tablespoons unsalted butter

1 cup whipping cream

2 tablespoons (or less) dark rum

1½ pounds grapes

1 ounce semisweet chocolate in block shape, such as Baker's

SERVING DISHES: 6 individual dessert saucers or glasses

PROCEDURE:

1. To make the cream, place brown sugar and water in saucepan and bring to a boil, stirring occasionally to help dissolve the sugar. Cook 1 minute.

2. Add butter and stir until it melts. Let mixture cool, then refrigerate until chilled. (Place in freezer to cool in a hurry.)

3. Whip cream until stiff. Whisk chilled brown sugar-butter mixture to blend, then add to whipped cream along with the rum. Stir or beat until sauce is well blended. Reserve in refrigerator until serving time.

4. Stem grapes, then wash and dry well. Seed, if necessary, then reserve in refrigerator until serving time.

5. Using a vegetable peeler, scrape shreds or curls from the chocolate. For curls instead of shreds, place chocolate in a sunny spot for a minute or microwave on high power for 30 seconds, then scrape. Reserve shreds or curls until serving time.

TO SERVE: Place grapes in serving dishes. Stir sauce to blend, then spoon over grapes. Sprinkle chocolate shreds or curls over tops. Serve.

DO-AHEAD INFORMATION: Grapes, sauce, and chocolate may all be prepared a day ahead.

GRAPES IN SHERRIED CREAM
(serves 6)

The glazed, sliced almonds sprinkled over this dessert at the end are what make it something really special. The sherried cream, however, is marvelous, a kind of easy, eggless, do-ahead zabaglione, the classic, Italian frothy dessert with egg yolks and Marsala wine. If you're serving big eaters, double the recipe for the sauce.

INGREDIENTS:
½ cup whipping cream
3 tablespoons cream sherry*
2 tablespoons powdered sugar
1½ pounds ripe, seedless white grapes
2½ ounces sliced almonds
2 tablespoons granulated sugar

*I used Cresta Blanca Triple Cream Sherry for this.

SERVING DISHES: 6 individual dessert saucers or glasses

PROCEDURE:

1. Whip cream until thickened but still runny. Add sherry and powdered sugar, then stir or beat to mix. Reserve in refrigerator until serving time.

2. Stem grapes and wash, if desired, and dry well. Reserve in refrigerator until serving time.

3. Place sliced almonds and granulated sugar in a heavy frying pan. Set pan over medium heat. The sugar will start to melt in about 4 minutes. Stir with a fork to coat the nuts with the sugar syrup. Let nuts and sugar cook, stirring now and then, until sugar caramelizes (turns brown) and nuts brown, about another 4 minutes. Don't worry if things start to smoke a little.

4. Turn nuts out onto a lightly greased baking sheet and allow to cool for 1 minute.

5. Using your fingers, separate the nuts and allow to cool another 5 minutes or so. Place right away in a plastic bag and store in the room.

TO SERVE: Place grapes in individual dessert saucers or glasses. Spoon sherried cream over and sprinkle glazed nuts on top. Serve.

DO-AHEAD INFORMATION: Cream and grapes may be done a day ahead. Nuts may be prepared a week or more ahead.

MIXED FRUIT IN CANTALOUPE RINGS
(serves 6)

This dessert is probably the most attractive one in this chapter. If you have managed to obtain a colorful array of fruits, the dish will be truly beautiful. Feel free to substitute other fruits for the ones listed, but try to choose the best color contrasts possible.

INGREDIENTS:

2 melons (cantaloupes or honeydews), 1½ pounds each or 5 inches in diameter
1 pint strawberries
1 pint blueberries

2 yellow peaches, unpeeled
2 tablespoons sugar
2 tablespoons orange liqueur (optional)
fresh mint leaf sprigs (optional)

SERVING DISHES: 6 dessert or salad plates, 8 inches in diameter

PROCEDURE:

1. Cut 3 slices, ½ to ¾ inch thick, from the center of each of 2 melons, reserving the ends. You will have 6 melon rings. It doesn't matter if the holes are not alike. Remove seeds from rings and cut off and discard rind. Reserve rings, covered, in refrigerator until serving time.

2. Using a melon ball scoop, cut balls of melon from the end pieces. Don't worry if the balls are not very round. Place in a bowl.

3. Brush and hull strawberries, then slice and add to melon balls.

4. Inspect blueberries, discarding stems and leaves. Wash (if desired), then dry and add to mixed fruits.

5. Cut peaches in half. Remove stones, then slice peaches into bite-size pieces and add to fruits.

6. Sprinkle sugar over fruits and stir well. There should be 6 cups or more. Add (optional) orange liqueur and stir again. Reserve in refrigerator until serving time.

TO SERVE: Place melon rings on dessert plates, then add 1 cup mixed fruit in center of each ring, letting fruits spill over onto edges of plates. Place (optional) sprigs of mint leaves around. You could serve sweetened, flavored whipped cream with this if you like.

DO-AHEAD INFORMATION: Melon rings and fruits may be prepared 6 to 8 hours ahead. You could prepare them a day ahead, but they would not be as fresh tasting.

SLICED PEACHES IN BLACKBERRY SAUCE
(serves 6)

If you like beautiful and unusual color mixtures, you will love this dessert. The deep yellow of the peaches and the magenta of the blackberry sauce are fascinating together. The taste combination is an excellent one, too.

INGREDIENTS:

1 17-ounce can blackberries in heavy syrup

1 teaspoon plain gelatin

¼ cup whipping cream (optional)

2 teaspoons powdered sugar (optional)

2 pounds ripe yellow peaches

2 to 3 tablespoons granulated sugar

SERVING DISHES: 6 individual dessert saucers or glasses

PROCEDURE:

1. Drain blackberries and reserve juice. Select 12 to 16 perfect berries and reserve in refrigerator until serving time. Place balance of berries (1 cup packed down) into container of food processor fitted with steel blade. Process to a purée, then reserve in processor.

2. Place blackberry juice (a scant cupful) in a glass container. Add gelatin and stir to mix, then allow 1 minute to soften. Microwave on high power for 1 minute or until gelatin has dissolved. (Or heat mixture in a small saucepan until almost boiling.)

3. Add gelatin mixture to blackberry purée in food processor. Process to mix. Pour into strainer over a bowl, then strain, discarding seeds.

4. Place blackberry mixture in refrigerator and allow to set 4 or 5 hours or overnight. To do this faster, place in freezer and allow 1½ hours to set.

5. Return jelled blackberry mixture to processor and process 30 to 60 seconds or until light in color and smooth. Reserve in refrigerator until serving time.

6. Wash peaches (peel them, if you prefer), then cut in half and remove stones. Cut peaches into bite-size pieces and place in a bowl. Add granulated sugar and stir to mix. Cover and reserve in refrigerator until serving time.

7. To prepare optional whipped cream topping, whip ¼ cup cream, then add ¼ cup blackberry mixture plus 2 teaspoons powdered sugar. Stir or whip, then reserve in refrigerator until serving time.

TO SERVE: Place sliced peaches into saucers or glasses. Beat blackberry sauce to make sure it is smooth, then spoon over peaches. Add a dollop of the blackberry whipped cream, if using, then place reserved whole blackberries on top. Serve.

DO-AHEAD INFORMATION: The blackberry sauce can be made one or two days ahead. The whipped cream sauce could be made early the day of serving and the peaches should be cut no sooner than 3 or 4 hours before eating. Both the sauce and the cream should be beaten again before serving.

PEACHES WITH BLUEBERRIES
IN RASPBERRY CREAM
(serves 6)

Here is another great summer combination, but with a sauce you can use all year round. Many people from different parts of the country tell me they never see fresh raspberries at all. For that reason, the sauce for this dessert is based on frozen ones, which are almost always available.

INGREDIENTS:
1 10-ounce package frozen red raspberries, packed in water and sugar

½ cup whipping cream
2 pounds fresh peaches
2–3 tablespoons sugar
1 pint fresh blueberries

SERVING DISHES: 6 individual dessert saucers or stem glasses

PROCEDURE:

1. Partially defrost package of frozen raspberries in room for ½ hour. (Or place package contents in bowl, cover, and microwave 1½ minutes on high power.)

2. Place raspberries and juice into container of food processor and process 15 seconds or until puréed. Reserve in machine.

3. Whip cream until stiff. Add raspberry purée and stir to mix. Cover and reserve in refrigerator until serving time.

4. Wash and dry peaches (optional: you may peel). Cut in half, remove stones, then slice peaches into bite-size pieces. Sprinkle with sugar, then stir.

5. Inspect blueberries, discarding leaves and stems. Wash, if necessary, and dry well. Add to peaches and stir to mix. Reserve in refrigerator until serving time.

TO SERVE: Place fruit into saucers or glasses. Spoon raspberry cream on top. Serve.

DO-AHEAD INFORMATION: Sauce may be done a day ahead. Stir or whisk before using. Prepare fruit no more than 4 to 6 hours before serving.

PEACHES WITH GRAND MARNIER WHIPPED CREAM
(serves 6)

Easy, fast, do-ahead, and delicious! Make sure the peaches are really ripe, which means you will probably want to buy them 3 or 4 days ahead to let them ripen. For a nice change, try sweet, white Babcock peaches if you can find them.

INGREDIENTS:

1 cup whipping cream

2–3 tablespoons Grand Marnier

2 tablespoons powdered sugar

2 pounds delicious, ripe peaches

2 tablespoons granulated sugar

SERVING DISHES: 6 individual dessert saucers or glasses

PROCEDURE:

1. Whip the cream until stiff but still runny. Add Grand Marnier and powdered sugar, then beat just to mix. Cover and refrigerate until serving time.

2. Wash peaches (peel if desired) and dry well. Cut into bite-size pieces and place in a bowl. Add granulated sugar and stir to mix. The sugar keeps the peaches from turning dark. Reserve in refrigerator until serving time.

TO SERVE: Place peaches in saucers or glasses, then spoon cream on top. Serve. For a nice extra touch, sprinkle glazed sliced almonds (see recipe for Grapes in Sherried Cream) on top.

DO-AHEAD INFORMATION: The cream may be prepared a day ahead. Stir or beat before using. Slice and sugar peaches no sooner than 4 to 6 hours before serving.

PEARS WITH CRANBERRY-ORANGE SAUCE
(serves 6)

This dessert features one of the nicest dessert sauces I have ever tasted, and it seems so easy as to be ridiculous. Both the lovely red color of the sauce and its wonderful tartness make it a perfect accompaniment to fresh pears.

INGREDIENTS:

1 16-ounce can jellied cranberry sauce

½ cup orange juice

6 ripe pears (Bartlett, Bosc, Comice, or other)

1 lemon

3 tablespoons sugar

SERVING DISHES: 6 individual dessert saucers

PROCEDURE:

1. Place cranberry sauce in a bowl and beat with an electric mixer for 1 minute or until smooth. Add orange juice and stir or beat until mixed. Reserve in refrigerator until serving time.

2. Three or 4 hours before serving, remove stems and fibers from pears and core, using a melon ball scoop. Rub cut surfaces with lemon. Place pears in a bowl and sprinkle with the sugar. Mix well, then reserve in refrigerator until serving time.

TO SERVE: Place 2 pear halves, cut side up (or down, if you prefer), in each dessert saucer. Spoon sauce over. If you like, you could accompany this with sweetened and flavored whipped cream.

DO-AHEAD INFORMATION: The sauce may be done 1 or 2 days ahead. The pears should not be prepared more than 3 or 4 hours before serving to be at their best.

PEARS WITH SOFT-FROZEN STRAWBERRY SAUCE
(serves 6)

Here is a good fall and winter dessert, thanks to the availability of frozen strawberries. In this dish, fresh pears are sliced and lightly sugared, then served with a sauce of semi-frozen strawberry ice. Choose pears that are ripe but still slightly green. The perfect pear should be hard over most of its surface, but when you push with your thumb near the stem, the flesh will give.

INGREDIENTS:

1 10-ounce package frozen sliced strawberries, packed with sugar
6 medium pears (2 pounds) (Bartlett, Bosc, Comice, or other)
lemon juice
2 tablespoons sugar

SERVING DISHES: 6 individual dessert saucers or glasses

PROCEDURE:

1. Leave frozen strawberries in room 30 minutes to slightly defrost. (Or put package contents in bowl, cover, and microwave 1½ minutes on high power.)

2. Place strawberries and their juice into container of food processor fitted with steel blade. Process to a purée. Transfer to a bowl, cover, and place in freezer. Bring out to room 30 minutes before serving.

3. Wash, then cut pears (unpeeled) in half, trimming away ends, stems, and fibers and removing cores with a melon ball scoop. Rub cut surfaces with lemon juice to keep from darkening.

4. Cut pears into bite-size pieces and place in a bowl. Sprinkle right away with sugar and toss well. The sugar also prevents the pears from darkening. Cover and refrigerate until serving time.

T O   S E R V E :   Place cut pears in saucers or glasses. Beat frozen strawberry mixture with a fork to return to sauce consistency (or rework in processor). Spoon semifrozen purée over pears. Serve.

D O - A H E A D   I N F O R M A T I O N :   Pears may be sliced and sugared up to 6 or 8 hours before serving. Strawberry ice may be done 1 or 2 days ahead or longer.

PINEAPPLE WITH CARROT-LIME CREAM
(serves 6)

The Carrot-Lime Cream in this dessert is wonderful as a topping for fruit and is particularly nice with fresh pineapple. When making it, be careful not to whip the cream too stiff as the sauce is better somewhat runny.

INGREDIENTS:

1 pineapple (3 to 5
    pounds)
2 tablespoons granulated
    sugar
1 medium carrot
    (2 ounces)

½ cup whipping cream
1½ tablespoons lime juice
    (or lemon)
⅓ cup powdered sugar

SERVING DISHES: 6 individual dessert saucers or glasses

PROCEDURE:

1. Peel, core, and cut pineapple into bite-size pieces. Place in a bowl. Sprinkle granulated sugar over, then stir, cover, and refrigerate until serving time.

2. Scrub carrot (optional: peel or scrape), then slice and microwave 1 minute on high power, or steam or boil until barely tender. Chop fine. Allow to cool.

3. Whip cream until thickened but still runny, then whisk in lime juice and powdered sugar. Add cooled, chopped carrot. Stir, then cover and refrigerate until serving time.

TO SERVE: Place pineapple pieces in saucers or glasses. Stir carrot cream, then spoon on top. Serve.

DO-AHEAD INFORMATION: Both the pineapple and the cream topping may be prepared a day ahead.

PINEAPPLE WITH COCONUT, BROWN SUGAR, AND RUM
(serves 6)

I had a simple yet magnificent dessert in Havana 33 years ago and the memory of it is as vivid as if it had happened yesterday. The dessert consisted of a slice of magnificent, ripened-on-the-stalk pineapple plus fresh coconut in syrup. The dessert that follows was inspired by that memory.

In pineapples, the bottom part is a lot sweeter than the top. If you can afford it, you might splurge and use the bottom parts of 2 different pineapples. If you decide to do this, serve the pineapple in slices, cored and with the core hole filled with the coconut mixture.

INGREDIENTS:

1 cup (packed) dark brown sugar

½ cup water

1 7-ounce package flake-style coconut (2 cups, packed)

1 pineapple, 4–5 pounds

2–3 tablespoons sugar

2 tablespoons rum

SERVING DISHES: 6 individual dessert saucers

PROCEDURE:

1. Place brown sugar and water in a saucepan. Bring just to the boil, stirring to dissolve sugar. Remove from heat and allow to cool to warm.

2. Stir coconut into brown sugar syrup in saucepan. Reserve in refrigerator until serving time.

3. Peel, core, and cut pineapple into bite-size pieces.

Place in bowl and sprinkle with sugar. Stir, cover, and refrigerate until serving time.

TO SERVE: Place pineapple pieces in saucers. Heat coconut and syrup, stirring slowly most of the time. Spoon a mound of coconut over each dessert; then, using the back of a spoon, make an indentation in each mound and place 1 teaspoon rum in it. Serve.

DO-AHEAD INFORMATION: Both the coconut mixture and pineapple may be prepared a day ahead.

PURPLE PLUMS CHANTILLY
(serves 6)

There are a few dishes in this book that are so simple it is hard to believe they are fabulous. This is one of them. It is a dish of sliced, sweet, perfectly ripe plums served with Creme Chantilly, whipped cream with powdered sugar and vanilla. There are two things that make this dessert fabulous: first, the quality of the plums. There is nothing quite like ripe, juicy, sugar-sweet plums at the peak of their season. Second is the simplicity of the dish. It takes nerve and daring to know and trust the quality of the fruit enough to let it be shown off with so little embellishment.

I cannot overemphasize that you must have sweet, wonderful, perfect plums. Get your produce man's cooperation on how far ahead to buy them to allow to ripen properly. The dish is truly divine if the plums are good and at that wonderful, magical moment of sweetness.

INGREDIENTS:

3 pounds plums (Santa
    Rosa or other)
2–3 tablespoons
    granulated sugar

1 cup whipping cream
2 tablespoons powdered
    sugar
1 teaspoon vanilla

SERVING DISHES: 6 individual dessert saucers or glasses

PROCEDURE:

1. Wash plums and dry well. Cut in half and remove pits. Slice plum halves into 2 or 3 wedge-shaped pieces and place in bowl. Do not slice them too thin. Sprinkle granulated sugar over and toss well. Cover and refrigerate until serving time.

2. Whip cream with powdered sugar until thick but still runny. Stir in vanilla. You have just made what the French call Creme Chantilly. Reserve, covered, in refrigerator.

TO SERVE: Serve chilled, right out of the refrigerator, or bring out to room 20 to 30 minutes ahead. Spoon plums into saucers or glasses, then top with the thick but still flowing Creme Chantilly.

DO-AHEAD INFORMATION: The Chantilly may be done a day ahead. Stir or whisk again just before serving. Prepare the plums 6 to 8 hours before serving.

STRAWBERRIES WITH CHOCOLATE CREAM AND CHOCOLATE SAUCE
(serves 6)

This dessert is excruciatingly good. How could it miss, with strawberries and chocolate and cream? The colors are gorgeous with the two browns and the red, and the dish tastes perhaps even better than it looks. As you have probably already gathered, I really like this.

INGREDIENTS:

⅔ cup cocoa
1 cup + 2–3 tablespoons
    sugar (total)
⅔ cup water
2 tablespoons unsalted
    butter
1 teaspoon vanilla
1 cup whipping cream
3 pints good, fresh
    strawberries

SERVING DISHES: 6 individual dessert saucers

PROCEDURE:

1. Place cocoa, 1 cup sugar, and water in a saucepan, then bring to a boil over medium heat, whisking all the time. Whisking continuously, let mixture foam up and cook for 2 minutes. Stir in butter and vanilla, then transfer to a bowl and let cool. This is the chocolate sauce.

2. Whip cream until stiff. Stir in ½ cup cooled chocolate sauce. This is the chocolate cream. Reserve both cream and sauce in refrigerator until serving time.

3. Three or 4 hours before serving, brush (or wash and dry well), hull, and slice strawberries. Place in a bowl. Sprinkle 2 or 3 tablespoons sugar on top and stir to mix. Reserve in refrigerator until serving time.

TO SERVE: Spoon sliced strawberries into saucers. Place ¼ cup chocolate cream on top center of each dessert. Dribble 1 tablespoon chocolate sauce over that, streaking it so that the chocolate cream shows through. Serve.

DO-AHEAD INFORMATION: Both chocolate sauce and cream may be done a day ahead. The strawberries should be prepared no sooner than 3 or 4 hours before serving.

STRAWBERRIES AND KIWIS IN COINTREAU FROZEN CREAM
(serves 6)

Here is a simple, refreshing, and beautiful dessert. The sauce for these lovely strawberries and kiwis is vanilla ice cream, semifrozen, mixed with Cointreau. You may use any orange liqueur for this, but I like Cointreau and Grand Marnier the best.

One of these days, when the California kiwi crop gets firmly established, the prices for this fascinating fruit will come down (they say) and this dish will no longer be so expensive.

INGREDIENTS:

2 pints strawberries
4 to 6 kiwis, depending upon size of fruit and your budget

2–3 tablespoons sugar
1 pint vanilla ice cream
2 tablespoons orange liqueur

SERVING DISHES: 6 individual dessert saucers

PROCEDURE:

1. Brush, hull, and slice strawberries into ³⁄₁₆-inch slices. Place in a bowl.

2. Cut off the two ends of the kiwis. Slip a teaspoon in between skin and flesh. Turning the spoon, remove and discard skin. Slice kiwis across into round, ³⁄₁₆-inch slices and add to strawberries. Sprinkle sugar over fruits, then stir, cover, and reserve in refrigerator until serving time.

3. Two or 3 hours before serving, transfer ice cream from freezer to refrigerator to allow to soften.

TO SERVE: Using an electric mixer or wire whisk, beat ice cream and orange liqueur until smooth, but still semifrozen. Place half of this sauce in bottoms of serving saucers, then add fruits and top with remainder of sauce in such a way as to allow the fruits to show. Serve.

DO-AHEAD INFORMATION: The fruits may be prepared 6 to 8 hours before serving. The ice-cream sauce should be assembled at the last minute.

STRAWBERRIES IN STRAWBERRY SOUR CREAM
(serves 6)

Strawberries and sour cream are one of life's great combinations. This fresh and luscious dessert features this delightful pair and is especially nice, partly because it isn't overly sweet. An extra dividend is that the sauce can be served in any season as it uses frozen strawberries.

INGREDIENTS:

1 10-ounce package frozen
   sliced strawberries,
   packed with sugar
8 ounces sour cream
1 tablespoon cold water

1 teaspoon plain gelatin
2–3 pints flavorful, fresh
   strawberries
2–3 tablespoons sugar

SERVING DISHES: 6 individual serving saucers or glasses

PROCEDURE:

1. To make the sauce, place frozen strawberries in a glass dish, then cover and microwave at high power for 1 minute. (Or let package of frozen berries sit at room temperature for 30 minutes.)

2. Place partially defrosted strawberries into container of food processor fitted with steel blade. Process 30 seconds or until it is a fairly smooth purée. Add sour cream and process another 15 seconds or until cream is somewhat smooth. Reserve in processor.

3. Place cold water in small glass. Add gelatin and stir to mix. Let soften 1 minute, then microwave at high for 30 to 60 seconds or until gelatin has dissolved. (Or dissolve in a metal cup placed in almost boiling water.)

4. Turn on food processor containing strawberry mixture, then pour hot gelatin mixture down feed tube rather fast. Process a few seconds or until mixed. Transfer to bowl and reserve in refrigerator until serving time.

5. Three to 4 hours before serving, prepare the fresh strawberries. Set aside 6 pretty, whole berries to be used at the end. Brush (or wash and dry well), hull, and slice berries and place in a bowl. Sprinkle sugar over, then stir and reserve in refrigerator until serving time.

TO SERVE: Place berries into saucers or glasses. If sauce has jelled, beat or process until runny again. Spoon over sliced berries, then add reserved whole berries on top. Serve.

DO-AHEAD INFORMATION: The sauce may be made a day ahead. The fresh strawberries should be hulled no more than 3 or 4 hours before serving.

2

COOKED FRUIT DESSERTS

BAKED APPLES WITH MARBLEIZED CRANBERRY SAUCE

BAKED APPLES WITH WALNUT BROWN SUGAR SAUCE

CRISP APPLE CRISP

WORLD'S BEST BLACK CHERRY COMPOTE

BLUEBERRY COMPOTE WITH GLAZED NUT TOPPING

PLUMPED FIGS IN HOT BUTTERED MINCEMEAT SAUCE

SLICED PEACHES IN PEACH SAUCE

PEACHES IN SPICED RED WINE

CHOCOLATE PEAR BETTY

PEAR SURPRISE WITH CHOCOLATE SAUCE

PEARS WITH RASPBERRY SAUCE

PLUM CRISP WITH OAT TOPPING

RHUBARB COMPOTE WITH FRESH STRAWBERRIES

As Chapter 1 featured summer fruits, Chapter 2 deals mainly with those of the winter. Two-thirds of the recipes in this section use apples, pears, raisins, and dried fruits—in short, the fruits that appear at the end of summer and are available throughout the fall and winter months.

Baking or poaching these winter fruits does something marvelous to them. If offered the choice between a raw apple and a piece of apple pie, most people would probably choose the pie. I know I would, assuming the pie is a good one. Something magical happens in cooking, especially with apples and pears, that almost seems to create brand-new products with little apparent relationship to the fresh fruits they once were. This chapter deals with that phenomenon.

Black cherries are definitely not a winter fruit, but I hope you will try the Black Cherry Compote, anyway. It involves a slightly different twist in fruit poaching that I think is wonderful. The fruit is not actually cooked, but is placed in hot syrup and allowed to cool in it. The results are fresh and delightful. The same technique is used for the Blueberry Compote. Try them both. Incidentally, in case you're interested, my favorite dish in this section is probably the Plumped Figs in Hot Buttered Mincemeat Sauce. I am loath to admit that it's also undoubtedly the one with the most calories.

BAKED APPLES WITH MARBLEIZED CRANBERRY SAUCE
(serves 6)

In this dessert, baked apples are served with a streaked red and white cranberry–whipped cream sauce that is one of the prettiest, easiest, and best-tasting sauces in this book. The dessert is topped with rosettes of sweetened whipped cream. While working on this dish, I was fascinated to discover that jellied purées can be turned into sauces by simply beating them, then thinning them out with a little liquid.

INGREDIENTS:

6 medium-large baking
    apples
1 tablespoon granulated
    sugar

1 16-ounce can jellied
    cranberry sauce
1 cup whipping cream
2 tablespoons powdered
    sugar

SERVING DISHES: 6 individual serving saucers

PROCEDURE:

    1. Preheat oven to 425 degrees.
    2. Wash apples, then core from the top using a melon ball scoop. Cut a slit in the skin all around the side of each apple to make a continuous ring. This keeps apples from

bursting open. Stand apples up in baking pan or dish. Sprinkle ½ teaspoon granulated sugar over each one.

3. Bake apples in preheated 425-degree oven 30 to 40 minutes or until tender. Test for doneness by poking with a fork. Cool, then chill.

4. Place cranberry sauce in a bowl, then beat with electric mixer 1 minute or until sauce is smooth.

5. Whip cream until starting to stiffen but still runny. Fold *half* of this into cranberry sauce, using only 4 or 5 strokes so that the sauce stays streaky or marbleized. Add powdered sugar to balance of cream and whip until stiff. Reserve sauce and whipped cream in refrigerator until serving time.

TO SERVE: Bring apples out to room 1 hour before serving. At serving time, place an apple in each saucer. Give chilled sauce a *few* more folding strokes in case it has separated, then spoon over tops and around bases of apples. Whip cream stiff again, then pipe rosettes on top.

DO-AHEAD INFORMATION: Both apples and sauce and whipped cream may be prepared a day ahead.

BAKED APPLES WITH WALNUT BROWN SUGAR SAUCE
(serves 6)

You bake apple halves for this delicious wintertime treat. And the sauce is a rich combination that lifts a simple and good dessert to the heights of fabulous.

INGREDIENTS:

¼ cup light corn syrup

½ cup dark brown sugar

½ stick (2 ounces)
   unsalted butter

½ cup walnuts, chopped
   coarsely

¼ cup seedless raisins

3 tablespoons milk or
   cream

6 baking apples (Rome
   Beauty, Golden
   Delicious, Granny
   Smith, or other tart,
   juicy cooking apples)

COOKING UTENSIL.   A 12¾ × 9 × 2-inch baking dish

PROCEDURE:

1. Place corn syrup, brown sugar, and butter in a saucepan and bring to a boil, stirring all the time. Remove from heat and stir or whisk another few seconds or until brown sugar has dissolved. Add nuts, raisins, and milk, then stir and allow to cool. Reserve in refrigerator until serving time.

2. Preheat oven to 425 degrees.

3. Cut apples in half, trim ends, then core with a melon ball scoop. Place apples in baking dish, cut side down. Bake in preheated 425-degree oven 10 to 12 minutes or until firm-tender. Allow to cool. Reserve in refrigerator until serving time.

TO SERVE: Place 2 apple halves in each of 6 individual dessert saucers, hole sides up. Put a spoonful of raisin-nut sauce in each hole. For a fancier touch, spoon or pipe sweetened whipped cream in the center. Serve chilled, room temperature, or warm.

DO-AHEAD INFORMATION: The apples may be done 1 or 2 days ahead, and the sauce a week ahead or more.

CRISP APPLE CRISP
(serves 6)

The first time I made a standard apple crisp, how disappointed I was when it turned out that it wasn't crisp at all.
In this version, the topping is truly crisp and this mostly
fruit dish is spicy and wonderful. I used Pippin apples for
this, but Cortland, Golden Delicious, or Granny Smith are
also good.

INGREDIENTS:

5–6 apples (2 pounds)
2 tablespoons sugar
½ teaspoon cinnamon
¼ teaspoon nutmeg
1 tablespoon lemon juice
½ cup dark brown sugar

¾ stick (3 ounces)
   unsalted butter, cut
   into ½-inch cubes
¾ cup all-purpose flour
¼ cup (1 ounce) walnuts,
   cut into ¼-inch dice

COOKING UTENSIL: An 8 × 8 × 2-inch glass baking dish
(not necessary to grease)

PROCEDURE:

    1. Preheat oven to 350 degrees.

    2. Cut unpeeled apples in half. Core with melon ball
scoop, then slice into wedges ½-inch thick at fattest part.
Place in baking dish in a heap.

    3. Mix sugar, cinnamon, and nutmeg, then sprinkle
over apples in dish. Add lemon juice and toss with a fork.
Pack down to level the top. Reserve.

    4. Place brown sugar and butter cubes in food processor
fitted with steel blade. Process until sugar and butter form
a smooth paste, then scrape out into a bowl.

    5. Add flour to this paste, then, using 2 knives, cut in

until white, floury look disappears but mixture is still crumbly. Stir in walnuts. Distribute in an even layer over apples.

6. Bake at 350 degrees for 45 to 50 minutes or until topping is nicely browned and apples are tender. Cool, then reserve in refrigerator until serving time.

TO SERVE: Serve warm, room temperature, or chilled. This is delicious just as it is, or you can pour a small pitcher of heavy cream over it. It isn't too bad with a little vanilla ice cream served on the side.

DO-AHEAD INFORMATION: May be made 1 or 2 days ahead. It also freezes well.

WORLD'S BEST BLACK CHERRY COMPOTE
(serves 6)

The reason for the immodest title of this dish is to call attention to an unusual poaching method. The normal way to poach cherries is to boil slightly unripe fruit in syrup until tender. In the method proposed here, ready-to-eat, full-flavored cherries are placed in hot syrup, then allowed to cool. This results in cherries that are at a delightful stage halfway between cooked and fresh.

In this compote, the specially poached cherries are served topped with sweetened whipped cream flavored with Cointreau, one of the world's best orange liqueurs. Cointreau and Grand Marnier, two great orange liqueurs, are quite different from each other in taste and aroma but are equally wonderful.

INGREDIENTS:

1½ pounds ripe Bing
   cherries
1 cup granulated sugar
2 cups water
1 teaspoon vanilla

1 cup whipping cream
2 tablespoons powdered
   sugar
2–3 tablespoons
   Cointreau*

SERVING DISHES: 6 individual serving saucers or glasses

PROCEDURE:

1. Remove stems and pits from cherries (there are inexpensive tools for this).

2. Place sugar and water in a saucepan. Bring to a boil, stirring occasionally to help dissolve sugar. Remove from heat and allow to cool for exactly 5 minutes.

3. Add vanilla, then place cherries in syrup and submerge. (Try placing over them a small bowl filled with raw rice sitting on a saucer.) Allow cherries to cool in the syrup, then reserve in refrigerator until serving time.

4. Whip cream with powdered sugar until thick but still runny. Add Cointreau. Reserve, covered, in refrigerator.

TO SERVE: Spoon cherries with some of their syrup into serving dishes. Top cherries with Cointreau cream, whipped again until thick but still slightly runny.

DO-AHEAD INFORMATION: Compote may be done 2 or 3 days ahead and kept in refrigerator. Cream may be prepared 6 to 8 hours ahead.

*You could substitute Grand Marnier or any orange liqueur, but taste as you go.

BLUEBERRY COMPOTE WITH GLAZED
NUT TOPPING
(serves 6)

The blueberries in this recipe are just barely cooked so that they hold their shape but their full flavor seems released. The walnut, oat, and brown sugar glazed topping is a wonderful concoction that you can sprinkle over a lot of different desserts. Don't be put off by the health-food sound of it. It's wonderful.

INGREDIENTS:

2 cups water
1 cup sugar
2 pints fresh blueberries
½ stick (2 ounces)
   unsalted butter

1 cup regular rolled oats
¼ cup dark brown sugar
2½ ounces walnut bits (1
   cup walnuts chopped
   in ¼-inch dice)

SERVING DISHES: 6 individual dessert saucers

PROCEDURE:

1. Place water and sugar in a saucepan and bring to a boil, stirring occasionally.

2. Inspect the blueberries, removing stems and leaves, then wash if necessary. When sugar and water are boiling and sugar is dissolved, add blueberries. Return to the boil, then remove from heat and let cool.

3. Heat butter in a large frying pan or sauté pan. Add oats, brown sugar, and walnuts, then cook over medium-low heat for 7 minutes, stirring about every 30 seconds. The oats will brown slightly. Spread on baking sheet and allow to cool. Store in plastic.

TO SERVE: Spoon blueberries and syrup into saucers. Sprinkle with glazed oats and walnuts. Serve. It wouldn't hurt this dessert if you slipped in a little Creme Chantilly (see recipe for Sliced Peaches in Peach Sauce, step 4) on top of the blueberries just before sprinkling over the topping.

DO-AHEAD INFORMATION: The blueberries could be done a day ahead. The oat-walnut topping could be done a week or more ahead.

PLUMPED FIGS IN HOT BUTTERED MINCEMEAT SAUCE
(serves 6)

Here is a good winter dessert that has me really excited. Dried figs are plumped, then served in a frothy, spicy mincemeat sauce with butter and rum. It's served hot with a scoop of vanilla ice cream on top, and the contrast in temperatures and the complex flavors make this a truly outstanding dish.

INGREDIENTS:

2 12-ounce packages dried figs*
4–5 cups water
½ cup sugar
1 9-ounce package condensed mincemeat†
1 tablespoon cornstarch
1 tablespoon cold water
2 tablespoons unsalted butter
1 egg
¼ cup rum
1 quart vanilla ice cream

*I used a supermarket brand labeled Dried Calimyrna Figs, but any figs will do.
†I chose Borden's None Such Condensed Mince Meat, as it seems to be in the markets all year. If using regular mincemeat, either fresh or canned, use approximately 16 ounces instead of 9; then in step 2, use only 2 cups of reserved fig juice instead of 3.

SERVING DISHES: 6 individual serving saucers

PROCEDURE:

1. Cut and discard stems from figs; place in a saucepan and cover with cold water plus an inch. Bring to a boil, then simmer uncovered 15 minutes. Add ½ cup sugar, then stir and simmer another 10 minutes. Drain, reserving juice; allow figs to cool and reserve in refrigerator until serving time.

2. Crumble mincemeat and place in saucepan. Add 3 cups reserved fig juice. Add cornstarch and 1 tablespoon cold water, mixed together. Bring to a boil, whisking all the time. Simmer 5 minutes, whisking occasionally. Place butter in slivers on top surface of sauce to prevent skin from forming. Cool, then reserve in refrigerator until serving time.

3. At serving time, bring sauce to a boil, then add figs. Cook 1 minute or until figs are heated through.

4. Beat egg for 2 minutes using electric mixer at high speed. Pour on top of sauce in saucepan. Remove from heat, then stir, allowing egg to cook in the hot sauce. Add rum and stir.

TO SERVE: Spoon figs and sauce into serving dishes. Place a scoop of vanilla ice cream on top of each dessert. Serve.

DO-AHEAD INFORMATION: Both figs and sauce may be done a day ahead up to the point described in steps 1 and 2.

SLICED PEACHES IN PEACH SAUCE
(serves 6)

This is peach shortcake without the shortcake. It is a peach lover's delight. And what's especially nice about it is that it is light enough to serve after a fairly heavy meal. Make it in the middle of summer when peaches are ripe, delicious, and inexpensive.

INGREDIENTS:

¼ cup + 3 tablespoons granulated sugar (total)

1 cup water

3 pounds ripe peaches (8 or 9)

1 cup whipping cream

2 tablespoons powdered sugar

1 teaspoon vanilla

SERVING DISHES: 6 individual serving saucers

PROCEDURE:

1. For the sauce, put ¼ cup sugar plus 1 cup water in a saucepan. Bring to a boil, stirring occasionally, then remove from heat and reserve.

2. Peel half the peaches (dip 15 seconds in boiling water to facilitate), then cut into small, bite-size pieces. Add to syrup in saucepan, then return to a boil and let simmer 1 or 2 minutes. Cool, then reserve in refrigerator until serving time. (If this doesn't look very "saucy," smash it up a little.)

3. Wash the rest of the peaches (or peel, if you prefer), then cut into bite-size pieces. Sprinkle 3 tablespoons sugar over and stir. Reserve in refrigerator until serving time.

4. Prepare Creme Chantilly. Whip cream and powdered

sugar until firm but still slightly runny. Stir in vanilla. Reserve in refrigerator until serving time.

TO SERVE: Place sliced fresh peaches in serving dishes. Spoon cooked peach sauce on top and finish with a dollop of Creme Chantilly. Serve.

DO-AHEAD INFORMATION: The peach sauce and the Creme Chantilly may be prepared 8 to 10 hours ahead. Slice the fresh peaches no more than 4 or 5 hours before serving.

PEACHES IN SPICED RED WINE
(serves 6)

A lovely dish to serve very cold on a hot summer day. Serve it in stem glasses, topped with whipped cream.

INGREDIENTS:
1 bottle (3 cups +) red
   wine (Gallo Hearty
   Burgundy is fine)
⅔ cup sugar
⅛ teaspoon nutmeg

6 thin slices lemon peel
⅛ teaspoon ground cloves
1 teaspoon cinnamon
2 pounds ripe peaches (5
   or 6)

SERVING DISHES: 6 individual stem glasses

PROCEDURE:
   1. Place all ingredients except peaches in a saucepan, then bring to a boil and simmer 5 minutes.
   2. Wash peaches (peel, if you prefer), then cut into bite-size pieces, but not too thin. Add all at once to simmer-

ing wine mixture. Remove from heat and allow to cool. Reserve in refrigerator until serving time.

TO SERVE: Spoon peaches into glasses, adding wine sauce to almost cover. Serve very cold. For a more festive and fabulous touch, pipe or spoon sweetened whipped cream on top, and finish off with a dash of cinnamon.

DO-AHEAD INFORMATION: May be finished and placed in glasses 8 to 10 hours ahead. If serving cream, whip it ahead of time with powdered sugar (and vanilla, if desired), then refrigerate. Spoon or pipe over desserts just before serving, adding a sprinkling of cinnamon.

CHOCOLATE PEAR BETTY
(serves 6)

Ever since I first tasted Poires Hélène I've loved the combination of pears and chocolate. A lot of other people seem to agree. This is a delicious home-style dessert, which may not be as elegant as its French cousin, but is chocolatey, crunchy, and thoroughly delectable.

INGREDIENTS:

6 ounces real semisweet chocolate morsels*
4 tablespoons sugar (total)
½ stick (2 ounces) unsalted butter
1 5½-ounce package Pepperidge Farm

Brownie Chocolate Nut Cookies
2½ ounces walnut chips (1 cup walnuts in ½-inch dice)
4 pears (1½–2 pounds), almost ripe

*I used Nestlé's.

COOKING UTENSIL: An 8 × 8 × 2-inch glass baking dish

PROCEDURE:
1. Preheat oven to 350 degrees.
2. Place chocolate, 2 tablespoons sugar, and butter, cut into pieces, into a bowl. Heat until melted, stirring occasionally, either in microwave or on stove top by placing bowl in almost boiling water. Reserve.
3. Using your hands, break cookies into coarse pieces about ½-inch square. Place in a large bowl, then add nuts and stir to mix.
4. Cut pears in half, then remove stems, fibers, and cores using a melon ball scoop. Cut pears into bite-size pieces, not too small. Add to broken cookies and nuts. Sprinkle 2 tablespoons sugar on top, then stir everything well. Pour chocolate-butter mixture over and stir again until everything is well mixed.
5. Dump into baking dish and pack down to form a fairly solid cake.
6. Bake in 350-degree oven 20 to 30 minutes or until pears are tender. Allow to cool, then reserve in refrigerator until serving time.

TO SERVE: I like to serve this right out of the refrigerator when the topping is really crunchy. It goes really well with vanilla ice cream.

DO-AHEAD INFORMATION: May be done completely 1 or 2 days ahead.

PEAR SURPRISE WITH CHOCOLATE SAUCE
(serves 6)

A spoonful of peanut butter is the surprise—and surprisingly good it is with the buttery pears. Top this with an easy and delicious chocolate sauce and you have a splendid cold-weather dessert. For a change, use almond or hazelnut butter, or a chocolate-nut butter called *gianduja,* all of which you can probably find in a specialty food shop.

INGREDIENTS:

6 ounces real semisweet
    chocolate morsels*
½ cup milk
⅓ cup sugar
2 tablespoons unsalted
    butter
1 teaspoon vanilla

2 29-ounce cans Bartlett
    pear halves in heavy
    syrup
6 tablespoons chunky
    peanut butter, no salt
    added, if possible

SERVING DISHES: 6 individual dessert saucers

PROCEDURE:

1. To make the sauce, place chocolate, milk, sugar, and butter in a saucepan and heat, just barely enough, whisking constantly, until mixture is melted and smooth. Remove from heat, stir in vanilla, then allow to cool. Reserve in refrigerator until serving time.

2. Drain syrup from pears, choosing the 12 prettiest halves. Remove a slice from the rounded side of each of 6 pear halves so that they will sit flat. Place these halves in serving dishes, hole sides up. Spoon 1 tablespoon peanut

*I used Nestlé's.

butter into each pear hole, then place a second pear half on top, hole side down, as if to form a whole pear. Reserve in refrigerator until serving time.

TO SERVE: Warm the chocolate sauce just enough so that it flows again. If the kids are not invited, you could add 1 tablespoon rum. If they are, it wouldn't hurt to serve a scoop of vanilla ice cream on the side.

DO AHEAD INFORMATION: The chocolate sauce may be done 2 or 3 days ahead. The pear sandwiches should be assembled no more than 8 to 10 hours before serving.

PEARS WITH RASPBERRY SAUCE
(serves 6)

This is a lovely dessert, and one fairly low in calories. It consists of drained, poached pears served with a lightly tart raspberry purée. The recipe calls for canned pears, but since the sauce is so easy and fast, you might want to go a step further and poach your own pears. Another touch to make this dessert more fabulous is to serve it with sweetened whipped cream plus glazed sliced almonds. To glaze almonds, follow the easy procedure for glazing pecans in the Brown Sugar English Cream recipe, substituting sliced blanched almonds for pecans.

INGREDIENTS:
1 10-ounce package frozen   packed with sugar
    red raspberries   and water

2 tablespoons cold water
1½ teaspoons plain
  gelatin

2 29-ounce cans Bartlett
  pear halves in heavy
  syrup

SERVING DISHES: 6 individual dessert saucers

PROCEDURE:

1. Partially defrost frozen raspberries. Either leave package in room for 30 minutes or place in glass bowl, cover, then microwave 30 seconds and let sit 5 minutes.

2. Place raspberries and juice in container of food processor fitted with steel blade. Process 1 minute or until a smooth purée. Reserve in machine.

3. Place water and gelatin in a small glass cup, then mix and let sit 1 minute. Microwave on high power for 30 seconds or heat in a metal measuring cup over a double boiler until boiling hot. Stir well with a rubber spatula.

4. Turn on food processor, then pour hot gelatin mixture down feed tube in a thin stream. Process 5 seconds more, then pour raspberry purée into a bowl (may strain out seeds, if desired) and reserve in refrigerator until serving time.

5. Select 12 pear halves, then drain and dry well. Place 2 halves, holes down, in each of the serving dishes. Reserve in refrigerator until serving time.

TO SERVE: Whisk jelled raspberry purée back to sauce consistency. Spoon over pear halves. Serve.

DO-AHEAD INFORMATION: Raspberry purée may be made 1 or 2 days ahead. Arrange pears in saucers not more than 4 or 5 hours before serving.

TO POACH PEARS: Bring 3 cups water plus 1½ cups sugar to a boil in a saucepan. Peel 6 pears (Bartlett, Bosc, or Winter Nellis, etc.; pears ideally should be still "green," but only 2 or 3 days short of ready to eat), leaving them whole. Rub pears with lemon juice to keep them from turning brown. Core from the bottom, using a melon ball scoop. Simmer pears in syrup 10 to 30 minutes, or until they test tender when poked with a fork in the thickest parts. Remove from heat, then add 1 teaspoon vanilla. Cool pears in syrup. Chill in refrigerator. May be prepared 2 or 3 days ahead. To serve, stand pears up in saucers, spooning raspberry purée around bases.

PLUM CRISP
(serves 6)

Plums are not used much in baking these days and it's a shame, because they are wonderful. Try to find early summer Santa Rosa plums to use for this dessert, choosing slightly underripe ones. Desserts made with them remind me of ones made with tart apples, because of the plums' tart skins. Later-in-the-season Italian "prune" plums work fine for this dish, also.

INGREDIENTS:
1½–2 pounds fresh plums
2 tablespoons sugar
½ teaspoon cinnamon
¼ teaspoon nutmeg
½ cup dark brown sugar
¾ stick (3 ounces)

unsalted butter, cut into ½-inch cubes
¾ cup all-purpose flour
¼ cup walnuts, ¼-inch dice
1 cup regular rolled oats

COOKING UTENSIL: An 8 × 8 × 2-inch glass baking dish

PROCEDURE:

1. Preheat oven to 350 degrees.

2. Cut plums in half, removing pits. Slice plums into wedge-shaped pieces measuring ½ inch at thickest part. Place in baking dish in a pile.

3. Mix sugar, cinnamon, and nutmeg, then sprinkle over plums in dish and toss well with a fork. Pack down to level top. Reserve.

4. Place brown sugar and butter in food processor fitted with steel blade. Process until sugar and butter form a smooth paste (could do this using an electric mixer or smearing with your hands), then scrape out into a bowl.

5. Add flour to this paste; then, using 2 knives, cut in until white, floury look disappears but mixture is still crumbly. Stir in walnuts and oats. Distribute mixture in an even layer over plums.

6. Bake at 350 degrees for 30 to 40 minutes or until plums are tender and topping is slightly browned.

TO SERVE: Serve warm, room temperature (take out of refrigerator 1 hour before serving), or chilled. You may want to serve this with whipped cream or vanilla ice cream.

DO-AHEAD INFORMATION: May be made a day ahead, and stored in refrigerator.

RHUBARB COMPOTE WITH
FRESH STRAWBERRIES
(serves 6)

Rhubarb and strawberries go together with a special magic. This dish shows off the combination in one of its simplest and most delicious forms. Rhubarb is baked and cooled, then mixed with sliced fresh strawberries. The dish is served with sweetened, flavored, softly whipped cream.

Fresh field rhubarb is the best product to use for this, but is available only in April and May. Hothouse and frozen rhubarb, which are around longer, work fine; however, they cook in less time, so be careful. Test frequently toward the end of the baking. If you overcook rhubarb, instead of lovely nice chunks, you end up with a bowlful of mush.

INGREDIENTS:

2 pounds rhubarb,
    medium stalks
1 cup granulated sugar
1 cup whipping cream

¼ cup powdered sugar
1 teaspoon vanilla
2 pints strawberries

COOKING UTENSIL: A 12¾ × 9 × 2-inch glass baking dish

PROCEDURE:

1. Preheat oven to 350 degrees.

2. Trim off and discard any leafy green parts of the rhubarb. Wash, then cut into 1-inch pieces and place in baking dish. Sprinkle sugar over and stir to mix.

3. Cover with foil and bake 30 minutes or until tender. Test by poking with a fork. Cool until warm, then reserve in refrigerator until serving time.

4. Whip cream with powdered sugar and vanilla until stiff but still runny. Reserve in refrigerator.

5. Three or four hours before serving, brush (or wash, if necessary, but dry well), and hull the strawberries. Set aside 6 whole berries to use as decoration. Slice balance of berries and place in a bowl. Carefully dump rhubarb with sauce over them and supercautiously mix together so as not to mash the tender rhubarb. Reserve compote and whole berries in refrigerator until serving time.

TO SERVE: Place rhubarb-strawberry mixture in individual dessert saucers or glasses. Whisk cream again, making it thick but still somewhat runny. Spoon over fruit. Add a whole strawberry on top of each dessert. Serve.

DO-AHEAD INFORMATION: Rhubarb may be baked 1 or 2 days ahead. Cream may be whipped 8 hours ahead. Slice and add strawberries to compote 5 or 6 hours before serving.

3

BAKED CUSTARDS AND PUDDINGS

SPICED CUSTARD WITH APPLES

BLACK CHERRY CUSTARD

OLD-FASHIONED BREAD PUDDING

RAISIN BREAD PUDDING WITH PEANUT BUTTER

FOUR FRUIT CUSTARDS WITHOUT MILK

BLUEBERRY CUSTARD

CRANBERRY CUSTARD

ORANGE CUSTARD

STRAWBERRY-RASPBERRY CUSTARD

Custards are among the most delicious and wholesome desserts in the world. This chapter includes some. The old things are the good things. These desserts are still fabulous and wonderfully good today.

In addition to the traditional custards in this chapter, I have come up with four fruit-based custards that are delicious and new. At least, I've never heard of them. They feature fruit juices and purées instead of milk, which is the liquid used in conventional custards. These juices and purées give wonderful, intense flavors to the resulting custards. They are marvelous little discoveries that you are going to like.

The fruit custards—and all custards in general—are best eaten the day they are made, although they are still good 1 or 2 days later. Fruit custards are a little less stable than milk custards. You may find some juices in the bottom of the dish, particularly if you keep them more than a day or two in the refrigerator. This is minor, however, and they taste so good that that will not bother you. My favorites of the fruit custards are the Blueberry and the Strawberry-Raspberry, and of the traditional custards, I like the Spiced

Custard with Apples and the Old-Fashioned Bread Pudding.

CUSTARD MAKING AND BAKING HINTS

Many of the custards in this chapter are baked in a "water bath." This means that the custard, in its dish, is placed inside a tin or another dish containing hot water. Custards that contain liquid and egg and no thickening or binding agent should not boil, or they will curdle. The purpose of the water bath is to keep the custard from boiling.

Just out of curiosity, one day I tried baking one of these custards without the water bath. I placed the custard dish on a baking sheet, hoping the sheet might deflect enough heat so the custard wouldn't boil. I looked in the oven about halfway through the baking time and found that the custard around the edges of the dish was boiling quite wildly while a 3-inch area in the center was as still and calm as a pond. Needless to say, I have used a water bath ever since.

When is a custard done? Many recipes instruct you to poke with a knife and to keep doing so until the knife emerges clean. For me, it never seems to come out clean until it's overdone. I stopped using this test a long time ago. I now use the *wiggle test*. When I think the custard may be set, I open the oven door for 2 seconds, just time enough to give the side of the custard dish a sharp poke with the wooden end of a rubber spatula. I then quickly close the door, and from the way the custard wiggled I make up my mind if it is set or not. If any part of the custard wiggled like water instead of Jello, I allow another 10 minutes of baking, then test again and continue until it looks completely set.

Here are a few final details about custards: They do not freeze well, as they tend to separate when defrosted. They are perishable and must be kept refrigerated. Even in the refrigerator, they should not be kept beyond 3 or 4 days.

SPICED CUSTARD WITH APPLES
(serves 6)

This is a delicious baked custard with apples, cinnamon, nutmeg, and caramelized sugar, a great winter dessert. I used Pippins, but any good cooking apple will do fine for this.

INGREDIENTS:

3–4 apples (1 pound)   3 cups milk
2 tablespoons butter   ¼ teaspoon cinnamon
½ cup sugar   ¼ teaspoon nutmeg
5 eggs

COOKING UTENSIL: An 8 × 8 × 2-inch ovenproof baking dish

PROCEDURE:
1. Preheat oven to 325 degrees.
2. Wash apples, then cut in half. Remove stems and blossom ends, then core with a melon ball scoop. Cut apples into bite-size pieces.
3. Heat butter in frying pan, then add apples. Cook over medium-high heat for 4 minutes, stirring occasionally. The

apples should brown nicely. Add sugar and stir to mix. Continue to cook another 3 or 4 minutes over high heat or until juices caramelize (turn brown) and almost start to burn. Turn out into baking dish. Do not wash the pan.

4. Warm the eggs by placing them, in their shells, in a bowl and covering them with hot water. Let sit 5 minutes. Place milk in the unwashed frying pan and stir to dissolve any caramel left in the pan. Heat the milk until warm but not hot. Break eggs and whisk in a bowl just to mix. Add the warm milk plus the cinnamon and nutmeg and whisk again just to mix. The spices will float on the top and look odd, but they are all right.

5. Place a baking sheet on center shelf of oven, then pour custard on top of apples in baking dish, on the sheet. Bake in preheated 325-degree oven 35 minutes or until a knife poked near the center comes out clean. Do not over-bake or custard can turn watery. Cool on a rack, then refrigerate.

TO SERVE: Serve chilled, room temperature, or warm, as is, or accompanied by cream, milk, or applesauce.

DO-AHEAD INFORMATION: May be done a day ahead. Reserve, covered, in refrigerator.

BLACK CHERRY CUSTARD
(serves 6)

This delicious cherry custard is a variation of a well-known French dessert called a *clafouti*. A true *clafouti* has flour in it, often comes in a crust, and is a peasant dish which can be just a little on the heavy side. Here is a lighter, easier version which I think you will like just as well. If fresh cherries are available, use 1½ pounds, pitted or not, as you like.

INGREDIENTS:

2 16½-ounce cans pitted Bing cherries in heavy syrup
6 eggs
3 cups milk

½ cup sugar
Zest of 1 orange
3 tablespoons orange liqueur*
1 teaspoon vanilla

COOKING UTENSILS: An 8 × 8 × 2-inch ovenproof baking dish plus a 12¾ × 9 × 2-inch baking tin to use as a water bath

PROCEDURE:

1. Preheat oven to 325 degrees.

2. Drain cherries, reserving juice for another use. Place cherries in bottom of baking dish. Reserve.

3. Warm eggs in shells, by placing in bowl and covering with hot water. Let sit 5 minutes.

4. Heat milk and sugar in saucepan until warm but not hot, stirring to dissolve sugar. Break eggs, then place in bowl. Add milk mixture, orange zest, liqueur, and vanilla. Whisk to mix, then pour over cherries in baking dish. Stir to mix.

5. Place 3 cups of hot water in the baking tin, then place the baking dish with the custard to fit inside the tin. Place this whole business in the preheated 325-degree oven and bake 45 to 50 minutes, or until a knife stuck 2 inches from

*If you can afford it, use Cointreau or Grand Marnier for this. You can use kirsch, which is more traditional.

the center comes out almost clean. Do not overbake. Allow to cool on a rack. Reserve in refrigerator until serving time.

TO SERVE: Serve as is, chilled, room temperature, or warm.

DO-AHEAD INFORMATION: May be prepared 1 or 2 days ahead. Keep refrigerated, as it is perishable.

OLD-FASHIONED BREAD PUDDING
(serves 6)

Here is an old-fashioned bread pudding that is amazingly quick to put together. I was tempted to add a Southern-style whiskey sauce or a French-style apricot jam sauce to make it seem more fabulous, but I couldn't do it. I think it's fabulous plain, just the way it is. When serving, I do pour a little milk or cream over it, but that's all.

INGREDIENTS:

½ 16-ounce loaf of French or Italian bread, fresh or stale

3½ cups milk

3 eggs

⅔ cup sugar

2 teaspoons vanilla

⅛ teaspoon salt

½ cup seedless raisins

¼ teaspoon cinnamon

COOKING UTENSIL: An 8 × 8 × 2-inch baking dish

PROCEDURE:

1. Preheat oven to 350 degrees.

2. Slice bread 1-inch thick, then pull each slice apart into irregular 1-inch chunks. Reserve.

3. Place milk, eggs, sugar, vanilla, and salt in a bowl, then beat using hand-held electric mixer for 30 seconds or until sugar is dissolved.

4. Add bread chunks to milk-egg mixture and stir to moisten the bread.

5. Place raisins in baking dish, then dump bread mixture on top and stir to mix. This should look rough, with bread chunks sticking up here and there. Sprinkle cinnamon on top.

6. Bake at 350 degrees for 45 minutes or until custard is set.

TO SERVE: Serve chilled, room temperature, or warm, as is or with milk or cream. Maybe I shouldn't, but I like this best really cold.

DO-AHEAD INFORMATION: This is best eaten the day you make it, but it can be done 2 or 3 days ahead and kept in the refrigerator.

RAISIN BREAD PUDDING WITH PEANUT BUTTER
(serves 6)

Most kids (and many adults) will find this fabulous. It's a straightforward, homey dessert but its taste is positively irresistible.

INGREDIENTS:

8 slices raisin bread   3 cups milk
   (optional: with   ½ cup sugar
   cinnamon)   3 eggs
6 tablespoons chunky   1 teaspoon vanilla
   peanut butter

COOKING UTENSIL: An 8 × 8 × 2-inch ovenproof glass
baking dish

PROCEDURE:

1. Preheat oven to 350 degrees.

2. Trim crusts (optional) from bread, then spread some-what sparingly with peanut butter. Place in bottom of baking dish in 2 layers, looking like sandwiches.

3. Place milk and sugar in a saucepan and heat until just warm, stirring to help dissolve sugar. Place eggs and vanilla in a bowl and beat with a fork just until mixed. Add to warm milk-sugar mixture in saucepan, then pour into baking dish around the bread. Let sit and swell 5 minutes, pushing "sandwiches" down into liquid now and then.

4. Put baking dish on baking sheet, place in 350-degree oven, and bake 35 minutes or until a knife poked in the center comes out clean. The pudding will be slightly puffed. Do not overbake or custard will become watery.

5. Allow to cool, then reserve in refrigerator until serving time.

TO SERVE: Serve chilled, room temperature, or warm in saucers, as is or with milk or cream poured over.

DO-AHEAD INFORMATION: May be done 1 or 2 days ahead.

BLUEBERRY CUSTARD
(serves 6)

Here comes another of my favorites, a marvelous-tasting dish. It is a nonmilk custard made of nothing but canned blueberries and eggs. As usual, when something is this easy and this good, there is a rub. You may have trouble finding canned wild Maine blueberries. No matter, the custard is almost as good using regular canned blueberries.

INGREDIENTS:

6 eggs

3 15-ounce cans wild

Maine blueberries, in heavy syrup

COOKING UTENSILS: An 8 × 8 × 2-inch ovenproof baking dish plus a 12¾ × 9 × 2-inch baking tin to be used as a water bath

PROCEDURE:

1. Preheat oven to 325 degrees. Prepare water bath by placing 3 cups hot water in baking tin and placing custard dish in the water in the tin.

2. Warm eggs by placing, in shells, in a bowl and covering with hot water. Let sit 5 minutes.

3. Drain blueberries, reserving juice (about 2½ cups). Inspect berries, discard stems, and place berries in baking dish. Heat blueberry juice in a saucepan until very warm, but not burning hot.

4. Break eggs and place in a bowl. Beat with a fork just until mixed, then slowly beat blueberry juice into the eggs. Pour over blueberries in baking dish and stir to mix. Bake in water bath in preheated 325-degree oven 50 minutes or until custard is set.

5. Remove custard from water bath, then let cool on a rack. Reserve in refrigerator until serving time.

TO SERVE: I love this chilled. It could be served with ice cream, sour cream, or sweetened, flavored whipped cream on top. If you have any left over, it's fabulous on cereal in the morning.

DO-AHEAD INFORMATION: This looks best on the first day, but it keeps in the refrigerator 2 or 3 days or more. The juice tends to separate out the longer it is kept. Keep refrigerated; it is perishable.

CRANBERRY CUSTARD
(serves 6)

This unusual dish would be a nice dessert for a Thanksgiving or Christmas dinner. It is a milkless custard with cranberries, absolutely delicious and easier than pie.

INGREDIENTS:

6 eggs

2 16-ounce cans
    whole-berry cranberry
    sauce*

½ cup orange juice or
    water

COOKING UTENSILS: An 8 × 8 × 2-inch ovenproof glass baking dish plus a 12¾ × 9 × 2-inch baking tin to use as a water bath

*I used Ocean Spray.

PROCEDURE:

1. Preheat oven to 325 degrees. Prepare water bath by placing 3 cups of hot water in the baking tin, then placing the baking dish in the water in the tin. Reserve.

2. Warm eggs in shells by placing in bowl and covering with hot water. Let sit 5 minutes.

3. Place cranberry sauce in a saucepan and add ½ cup juice or water. Heat, stirring to break up lumps, until mixture is very warm but not burning hot.

4. Break eggs and place in a bowl. Beat with a fork just to mix, then slowly stir in cranberry mixture. Pour into baking dish, then place custard in water bath into preheated oven. Bake at 325 for 40 minutes or until custard is set.

5. Remove custard dish from water bath and allow to cool on rack. Refrigerate until serving time.

TO SERVE: Serve chilled in dessert saucers, as is or accompanied by ice cream, sweetened, flavored whipped cream, or plain cream.

DO-AHEAD INFORMATION: May be done 1 or 2 days ahead.

ORANGE CUSTARD
(serves 6)

This is particularly delicious when made with good, sweet oranges at the peak of the season. In addition to orange juice, the custard has 3 cups of orange slices in it so there is a strong orange flavor plus some chewy texture. It is refreshing and wholesome and one of my favorites.

INGREDIENTS:

7 eggs   2 cups orange juice
5 oranges (California   ½ cup sugar
    Navels or Florida
    Temples)

COOKING UTENSILS: An 8 × 8 × 2-inch ovenproof baking dish plus a 12¾ × 9 × 2-inch baking tin to be used as a water bath

PROCEDURE:

    1. Preheat oven to 325 degrees. Prepare water bath by placing 3 cups hot water in baking tin and placing custard dish in the water in the tin. Reserve.

    2. Warm eggs by placing, in shells, in a bowl and covering with hot water. Let sit 5 minutes.

    3. Slice tops and bottoms from oranges, using a large sharp knife and cutting in far enough to slice into the meat. Stand oranges up, then cut down, all around, cutting away rind and membrane. Cut oranges lengthwise into quarters, then reassemble the halves and slice across into ⅜-inch pieces. You should have a generous 3 cups. Place in baking dish and reserve.

    4. Place orange juice and sugar in a saucepan. Heat, stirring, until very warm but not burning hot.

    5. Break eggs and place in a bowl. Beat with a fork just to mix, then slowly stir in orange juice mixture. Pour over orange pieces in baking dish and stir to mix. Place custard and water bath in preheated 325-degree oven and bake 50 minutes or until custard is set.

    6. Remove custard from water bath and let cool on a rack. Reserve in refrigerator until serving time.

TO SERVE: Serve chilled, room temperature, or warm, as is. It may also be served with ice cream, sour cream, sweetened, flavored whipped cream, or plain cream.

DO-AHEAD INFORMATION: May be done 1 or 2 days ahead. Keep refrigerated; it is perishable.

STRAWBERRY-RASPBERRY CUSTARD
(serves 6)

This dessert is a real winner; it is smashingly good. It is the final dessert of a series of milkless fruit custards and unless you happen to be as goofy over wild Maine blueberries as I am, you will like it the best. If you think of it, allow the berries to defrost overnight in the refrigerator. If you should forget, defrost in the microwave.

INGREDIENTS:

6 eggs

2 10-ounce packages frozen sliced strawberries, packed with sugar

2 10-ounce packages frozen raspberries, packed with sugar and water

COOKING UTENSILS: An 8 × 8 × 2-inch glass ovenproof dish plus a 12¾ × 9 × 2-inch baking tin for use as a water bath

PROCEDURE:

1. Preheat oven to 325 degrees. Prepare water bath by placing 3 cups hot water in baking tin and placing custard dish in the water in the tin. Reserve.

2. Warm eggs by placing, in shells, in a bowl and covering with hot water. Let sit 5 minutes.

3. Place entire contents of 4 defrosted packages of frozen strawberries and raspberries in a saucepan. Heat, stirring, until very warm but not burning hot.

4. Break eggs and place in a bowl. Beat with a fork just until mixed, then slowly add strawberry-raspberry mixture, stirring it into the eggs. Pour into baking dish, then place with water bath in preheated 325-degree oven and bake 40 minutes, or until custard is set.

5. Remove custard from water bath and let cool on a rack. Reserve in refrigerator until serving time.

TO SERVE: Serve chilled, room temperature, or warm, as is. Ice cream, sour cream, sweetened, flavored whipped cream, or plain cream may be added.

DO-AHEAD INFORMATION: May be prepared 1 or 2 days ahead. Keep refrigerated; it is perishable.

4

CREAMS AND MOUSSES

BANANA MACAROON ENGLISH CREAM

BROWN SUGAR ENGLISH CREAM WITH GLAZED PECANS

CHOCOLATE ENGLISH CREAM WITH BANANA CHIPS

CHOCOLATE MARQUISE SURPRISE

LEMON CREAM WITH WHITE RAISINS IN GRAND MARNIER

LIME MOUSSE WITH CANDIED PEEL

PECAN PRALINE CREAM

TANGERINE MOUSSE

TWO-LAYERED RASPBERRY MOUSSE

The mousses and creams (the French call them *crèmes*) in this chapter are smooth, elegant, delicious, and beautiful. Yes, they are fabulous, too. The English creams and the fruit mousses are perfect ways to top off light luncheons or dinners, particularly these days when we all have a half an eye on our waistlines. It may surprise you to learn that most of the creams and mousses in this chapter (but not the two chocolate ones) are relatively low in fat and calories. I'm not saying that they are diet food, but I have worked very hard on them to keep down the fat and sugar content while keeping up the flavor and texture.

At a dinner for six recently, I served four of these mousses for a tasting. (If you want to make your friends happy, try the idea of serving more than one dessert yourself!) Anyway, I asked my guests to rank the desserts. It was almost a tie for first place among the Two-Layered Raspberry Mousse, Pecan Praline Cream, and Lime Mousse, with the Raspberry coming in slightly ahead of the others. What I found a little disconcerting was that the Tangerine Mousse was not as high on anyone's list as it was on mine. To me it's lovely—the truest, lightest, and most refreshing. But these are all so good, it really is hard to choose.

BANANA MACAROON ENGLISH CREAM
(serves 6)

Here is a home-style cream that will be applauded by your guests. Chewy coconut macaroons are diced, mixed with sliced bananas, and covered with a vanilla English Cream. It's a good-tasting, wholesome dish. Any good-quality soft coconut or almond macaroon will do for this, but I recommend Pepperidge Farm Coconut Macaroon Snack Bars. Except for being a little heavy on sugar and corn syrup, they are amazingly free of other additives.

INGREDIENTS:

2 cups milk (total)
6 egg yolks
⅓ cup sugar
2 teaspoons vanilla

3 Pepperidge Farm
    Coconut Macaroon
    Snack Bars (4½
    ounces)*
2 bananas

SERVING DISHES: 6 stem glasses or individual dessert saucers

PROCEDURE:

1. Have ready on the side ½ cup cold milk, a clean bowl, and a rubber spatula. Place remaining 1½ cups milk, yolks, and sugar in a saucepan (preferably heavy). Over medium-high heat, whisking occasionally, heat until mixture feels very warm to the touch. Continue cooking, but now whisking all the time, until mixture comes to the *first signs* of a boil (about 4 minutes). You will have to stop whisking now and then to see if there is any bubbling.

*These bars come 6 to a 9¼-ounce package. Serve the rest of the bars for another dessert or eat them.

When you see slight bubbles around the edges, immediately whisk in reserved ½ cup cold milk, then pour mixture into clean bowl. With rubber spatula, scrape any curdled part from the bottom of the pan and add to mixture. Stir in vanilla. Place uncovered in freezer for 1 hour.

2. Cut macaroon bars into ¼-inch dice. Divide evenly into 6 glasses or saucers.

3. When the English Cream is chilled, cut the bananas into ⅜-inch dice and add to macaroon pieces in the glasses. Pour about 3 tablespoons of the English Cream into each glass, then carefully stir so as not to dirty the sides of the glasses. Pour the rest of the cream into each glass. Refrigerate until serving time.

TO SERVE: Serve chilled as is or with sweetened, flavored whipped cream.

DO-AHEAD INFORMATION: The English Cream may be done 1 day ahead. Assemble the desserts on the day they are to be served. Keep refrigerated, covered with plastic, until serving time. This dessert is perishable. Do not keep more than 2 or 3 days, even in the refrigerator.

BROWN SUGAR ENGLISH CREAM WITH GLAZED PECANS
(serves 6)

This is a great favorite of mine partly because it features brown sugar and pecans, both of which I love. Also, the combination of textures in this dish—the smooth, cold cream and the chewy, caramelized nuts—makes it something really special.

INGREDIENTS:

2 cups milk (total)

6 egg yolks

1 cup (packed) dark
    brown sugar (total)

1½ teaspoons vanilla

½ stick (2 ounces)
    unsalted butter

4 ounces (1⅓ cups) pecan
    halves (smaller ones
    are prettier)

2 tablespoons water

SERVING DISHES: 6 individual stem glasses or dessert saucers

PROCEDURE:

1. Have ready on the side ½ cup cold milk, a clean bowl, and a rubber spatula. Place 1½ cups milk, yolks, and ¾ cup brown sugar in a saucepan (preferably heavy). Over medium-high heat, whisking occasionally, bring just to the *first signs* of a boil (about 4 minutes). Immediately whisk in reserved ½ cup cold milk, then pour mixture into clean bowl. With rubber spatula, scrape any curdled part from the bottom of the pan and add it to mixture. Add vanilla and butter, cut into pieces, and whisk until butter melts.

2. Pour into glasses or saucers and allow to cool, then chill in refrigerator for 5 or 6 hours or overnight. Do not cover until mixture is cold.

TO SERVE: Serve chilled as is, or with the following brown sugar–glazed pecans.

PROCEDURE FOR BROWN SUGAR–GLAZED PECANS:

1. Lightly butter a baking sheet and set aside.

2. Put ¼ cup brown sugar plus 2 tablespoons water into

a saucepan and place over medium-low heat. Bring to a boil, stirring to dissolve sugar. When sugar has dissolved and mixture is boiling, increase heat to medium high and do not stir any longer. Let syrup bubble hard for exactly 1 minute. Dump in the nuts and stir with a fork.

3. Change heat to medium low. Continue to cook while stirring for another 3 or 4 minutes. The nuts will brown and will start to smoke as if they were burning, which they are, but keep cooking and stirring. After smoking has gone on for 1 minute and nuts are somewhat browned, dump out on buttered baking sheet.

4. Separate nuts using 2 forks, then allow to cool. Store in plastic.

DO-AHEAD INFORMATION: The Cream may be done 1 or 2 days ahead and kept refrigerated. *Caution:* Do not keep longer, as this dessert is perishable. The pecans may be prepared a week ahead or longer. Store air-tight.

CHOCOLATE ENGLISH CREAM
WITH BANANA CHIPS
(serves 6)

This is a softly set chocolate cream dessert with a good, real chocolate taste. In looking for a garnish for this dessert, I happened upon banana chips, which I had seen around for a long time but had never tried. My, they're crunchy and good, and very pretty. Try to find the ones with no artificial flavor added. If you can't find them at all, use chocolate curls instead (see Grapes in Rum Butterscotch Cream).

INGREDIENTS:

2 cups milk (total)
6 egg yolks
1 cup minus 2 tablespoons
    sugar

1 teaspoon vanilla
2 ounces unsweetened
    chocolate
6 ounces banana chips

SERVING DISHES: 6 individual stem glasses or dessert saucers

PROCEDURE:

1. Have ready on the side ½ cup cold milk, a clean bowl, and a rubber spatula. Place 1½ cups milk, yolks, and sugar in a saucepan (preferably heavy). Over medium-high heat, whisking occasionally, heat until mixture feels very warm to the touch. Continue cooking, but now whisking all the time, until mixture comes to the *first signs* of a boil (3 to 4 minutes). You will have to stop whisking now and then to see if there is any bubbling. When you see slight bubbles around the edges, immediately whisk in reserved ½ cup cold milk, then pour mixture into clean bowl. With rubber spatula, scrape any curdled part from the bottom of the pan, adding it to mixture. Whisk in vanilla.

2. Chop the chocolate into coarse pieces and place in a bowl. Add ½ cup of the hot mixture to the chocolate and whisk until melted and smooth. Dump chocolate mixture into balance of hot cream, then whisk until mixed. Put into glasses or saucers (a generous ½ cup in each). Reserve in refrigerator until serving time.

TO SERVE: Just before serving, add banana chips to desserts. For a fancier touch, serve sweetened, flavored whipped cream on top with the banana chips placed around the sides.

DO-AHEAD INFORMATION: The Cream may be done 1 or 2 days ahead and kept, covered, in the refrigerator. Do not keep longer, as this dessert is very perishable even when chilled.

CHOCOLATE MARQUISE SURPRISE
(serves 6)

Well, here it is, the ultimate chocolate dessert.* A chocolate mousse with twice the normal amount of chocolate, it is rich, suave, creamy, dense. The surprise is a purée of dried figs hidden inside. The figs are a nice taste and texture contrast and give you strength to go on. I am also convinced that those grainy fig seeds help push all that cholesterol through. If you like neither surprises nor figs, you may leave this part out.

INGREDIENTS:

10 dried figs (6 ounces)
⅓ cup milk
4 eggs
8 ounces semisweet
    chocolate†

¾ stick unsalted butter (3
    ounces)
4 tablespoons sugar
2 tablespoons orange
    liqueur
1 teaspoon vanilla

SERVING DISHES: 6 stem glasses or dessert saucers

*This dish is not foolproof. Special egg-white beating and folding skills would be helpful.
†I used Nestlé's real semisweet chocolate morsels (approximately 2 cups).

PROCEDURE:

1. Remove stem ends, then place figs in container of food processor fitted with steel blade. Process 30 seconds or until purée comes together in a ball. Add milk and process until incorporated. Place rounded tablespoonfuls into serving glasses or saucers. Reserve.

2. Place eggs in shells in a bowl, then cover with hot water. Let sit 5 minutes.

3. Place chocolate, butter, and 2 tablespoons sugar in a 1-quart ovenproof beaker, then microwave for 2 minutes on high, or heat over double boiler until melted. Whisk until smooth. Separate eggs, placing whites in a bowl and adding yolks to chocolate mixture along with orange liqueur and vanilla. Whisk or beat this mixture until smooth and shiny.

4. Add 2 tablespoons sugar to whites, then beat at high speed with a hand-held electric mixer for 1 minute, or until whites are fairly stiff. Do not overbeat. Dump half the whites into the chocolate mixture and roughly mix in. Add balance of whites, then fold in quickly but carefully. Pour into glasses on top of fig purée. Refrigerate until serving time.

TO SERVE: Serve chilled, as is, or with sweetened, flavored whipped cream on top.

DO-AHEAD INFORMATION: May be done 1 or 2 days ahead. Cover with plastic and keep in refrigerator. This is very perishable.

LEMON CREAM WITH WHITE RAISINS IN GRAND MARNIER
(serves 6)

This is a pleasant and charming lemon cream. In classic French circles, it would be known as a Lemon Crème St. Honoré, except that instead of adding whipped cream at the end, in order to make the dessert lighter, I have added a whipped, jelled milk mixture. The addition of raisins soaked in Grand Marnier makes the dessert even more interesting and delicious.

Start this dessert a day ahead or the morning of the dinner, as there are two mixtures to be chilled and set.

INGREDIENTS:

½ cup seedless raisins (white preferred)

2 tablespoons water

2 tablespoons orange liqueur

6 egg yolks

¾ cup sugar

3 tablespoons cornstarch

3 cups milk (total)

3 tablespoons butter, cut into pieces

Zest of 1 lemon

½ cup lemon juice

1 slightly rounded teaspoon plain gelatin

SERVING DISHES: 6 stem glasses or individual dessert saucers

PROCEDURE:

1. Place raisins and water in a 1-quart ovenproof glass beaker. Cover and microwave 1 minute on high power, or bring to a boil in a small saucepan. Drain and discard juice, then add orange liqueur. Cover and reserve.

2. Place yolks and sugar in a bowl and whisk to mix. Add cornstarch and whisk again until mixed.

3. Place 2 cups milk in a saucepan and bring to a boil. Add half the hot milk to the yolk mixture and whisk to mix, then dump this back into the saucepan. Return to the boil, whisking over medium heat, then lower and let mixture burp and bubble for 3 minutes, whisking almost continuously. Remove from heat, then add butter, zest, and lemon juice. Whisk until butter melts. Dump into a bowl. Place on rack and cool 10 minutes, stirring occasionally to keep skin from forming. Place plastic in contact with top, then refrigerate several hours or until chilled.

4. Place gelatin plus ½ cup milk into 1-quart ovenproof beaker. Mix, then let sit 1 minute. Microwave 1 minute on high, or bring to a boil in a small saucepan, then whisk to mix and add remaining ½ cup milk. Whisk, then place in refrigerator 1 or 2 hours or until chilled and set.

5. Divide raisins and orange liqueur into the glasses or saucers. Beat the lemon cream with a wooden spoon until more or less smooth (it will not be perfect). Do not be tempted to beat this with a whisk or electric mixer or mixture can turn runny. Beat milk gelatin with an electric mixer or whisk until very smooth. This will not fluff up like whipped cream, but will get very smooth. Add to lemon mixture and beat with spoon (do not whisk) until fairly smooth. Spoon half the mixture into the glasses. Stir to mix in the raisins and liqueur, then top with the rest of the cream. Reserve in refrigerator until serving time.

TO SERVE: Serve chilled as is or, for an added touch, top with sweetened, flavored whipped cream.

DO-AHEAD INFORMATION: May be done completely 1 or 2 days ahead. Keep covered with plastic in refrigerator.

LIME MOUSSE WITH CANDIED PEEL
(serves 6)

Here is an elegant, smooth mousse with a wonderful, intense lime flavor. The candied peel adds a lovely finishing touch, as well as great texture, to the dish; however, it can be left out if you want an easier, faster dessert.

This dessert is a little on the tart side, which is the way most of my friends (but not all) like it. If you tend to like desserts a little sweeter, reduce the amount of lime juice in the recipe from ½ to ⅓ cup.

INGREDIENTS:

3–4 medium-large limes*
1¼ cups sugar (total)
1 cup whipping cream
Grated zest of 1 lime

1 envelope plain gelatin
5 or 6 ice cubes
(equivalent to ½ cup water)

SERVING DISHES: 6 stem glasses

PROCEDURE:

1. Using a vegetable peeler, remove wide strips of peel, not too thin, from 3 of the 4 (or 2 of the 3) limes. Cut each strip into julienne (skinny threads), 1/16- to ⅛-inch wide. Bring 3 cups water to a boil in a small saucepan, then add

*You may substitute 2 or 3 medium lemons for this to make a lemon mousse.

the peel and boil 10 minutes or until tender. Chew on one to test. Drain, rinse, and reserve.

2. Put ½ cup sugar plus ½ cup water into a saucepan. Bring to a boil, stirring occasionally to dissolve sugar. Add peel and return to a boil. Transfer to a small bowl, then refrigerate. Cover when chilled.

3. Grate zest from remaining lime. Squeeze limes to obtain ½ cup juice. Add zest to juice and reserve.

4. Beat cream until stiff but not overbeaten. Reserve in refrigerator.

5. Mix ¼ cup cold water with gelatin in a 4-cup glass beaker. Cover and microwave 1 minute or heat in metal measuring cup over double boiler until boiling hot. Stir well with rubber spatula, then add ¾ cup sugar, lime juice–zest mixture, and stir again until sugar is dissolved.

6. Right away, place ice cubes in container of food processor fitted with steel blade. Process until ice is grated coarsely. Add lime mixture and process 10 seconds or until mixed. Add reserved whipped cream and give machine 5 or 6 one-second pulses to mix.

7. Pour quickly (mixture is on the verge of setting) into 6 serving glasses.* Refrigerate. May be eaten right away or chilled until firmer.

TO SERVE: Just before serving, fish out small piles of the peel and place some on each dessert.

DO-AHEAD INFORMATION: The candied peel may be done a week ahead and kept, covered, in the refrigerator. The mousse may be done 1 or 2 days ahead or more and kept, covered, in the refrigerator.

*If the mixture sets too fast, transfer to a bowl and place in hot water. Stir or whisk until pourable again.

PECAN PRALINE CREAM
(serves 6)

This is a lovely English Cream flavored with pecan praline powder. Serve in individual stem glasses with coarse-chopped praline sprinkled on top. A rosette of whipped cream is piped on top of each dessert with a caramelized pecan half placed in the center. It is a beautiful, glamorous, and wonderful-tasting dessert.

INGREDIENTS:

Unsalted butter to grease tin

1 cup granulated sugar

¼ cup water

4 ounces pecans (1 cup halves), including 6 large halves for decoration

2 tablespoons cold water

1 envelope plain gelatin

2½ cups milk

6 yolks

1½ teaspoons vanilla

½ cup whipping cream

1 tablespoon powdered sugar

SERVING DISHES: 6 stem glasses

PROCEDURE:

1. Rub a baking sheet and a small plate with butter and set aside.

2. Place granulated sugar and ¼ cup water in a saucepan and bring to a boil over medium heat, stirring now and then to help completely dissolve the sugar.

3. Add pecans, then increase heat to high. Do not stir anymore, but you may swirl the pan to mix as it begins to color. Clean off the sides of the pan with a wet brush 1 time. Cook about 5 minutes or until sugar syrup is smoking and

has turned a good, rich brown color.* Pour onto buttered tin.

4. Right away, using 2 forks, pick out 6 perfect pecan halves and place on buttered plate. Allow to cool, then reserve in plastic. Allow balance of nuts and caramel to cool, but loosen from sheet with a spatula before completely cooled.

5. With a heavy knife, cut off about ¼ of the caramel-nut mixture and chop into ¼-inch dice. Wrap in plastic and reserve. Process balance of pecan-caramel in food processor until ground fairly fine to make powder. Reserve in plastic.

6. To make the Cream, have a clean bowl and a rubber spatula ready on the side. Place 2 tablespoons cold water in a small container. Sprinkle gelatin on top, then whisk to mix and reserve.

7. Place milk and yolks in a saucepan and add ground praline. Whisk to break yolks, then bring to the *first signs* of a boil (about 5 minutes), whisking occasionally, then more or less continuously as mixture gets very hot. Pour into clean bowl. With rubber spatula, scrape any curdled part from the bottom of the pan and add it to the mixture. Stir in the gelatin disk plus the vanilla, then whisk well to dissolve the gelatin. Pour into serving glasses. Refrigerate 4 or 5 hours or overnight.

8. Beat cream with powdered sugar until stiff. Reserve in refrigerator.

TO SERVE: Sprinkle reserved coarse-chopped praline over desserts, then pipe a large whipped-cream rosette in center of each. Place reserved caramelized pecan half on top. Serve.

*The trick here is to let the syrup get as brown as possible so as to give a nice caramel flavor; but at this point the syrup is actually burning, so you must be careful not to let it get so dark that it has a burned taste.

DO-AHEAD INFORMATION: Praline may be done weeks ahead and stored air-tight in room. Cream may be prepared 1 or 2 days ahead and kept in serving glasses, wrapped in plastic, in refrigerator. Desserts may be garnished and stored, uncovered, in refrigerator 4 or 5 hours before serving.

TANGERINE MOUSSE
(serves 6)

The secret of success in making this light, delicious mousse is to find sweet tangerines with lots of character. Diced pieces of fruit are added to the mousse for texture and richer flavor, while whipped-cream rosettes add a touch of class. This is both a lovely dessert and a fresh and pure one.

INGREDIENTS:

1 cup whipping cream
3 pounds medium-large tangerines*
2 tablespoons cold water
1 envelope plain gelatin
1 tablespoon granulated sugar

2 or 3 very small sweet tangerines (2 inches or less in diameter)
3 tablespoons powdered sugar (total: 2 optional)

SERVING DISHES: 6 stem glasses

*I tried this recipe using frozen tangerine juice instead of freshly squeezed and didn't like it at all.

PROCEDURE:

1. Beat cream until stiff. Reserve in refrigerator.

2. Peel 2 tangerines, pulling apart into segments. Using a sharp knife, with the segment flat on a cutting board, cut across the low, seedy area (the part that was formerly at the center of the tangerine), removing a strip of the tough membrane (to be discarded) and opening up the segment. Scrape out seeds, then cut segments across into 5 or 6 pieces. Reserve in refrigerator.

3. Squeeze enough of the rest of the tangerines to get 1½ to 2 cups juice. Reserve.

4. Place cold water in a 4-cup glass beaker. Sprinkle gelatin on top and whisk to mix. Cover with plastic and microwave on high for 30 seconds or heat in metal measuring cup over double boiler. Stir well with a rubber spatula, then stir in granulated sugar and stir until dissolved. Add ¼ cup tangerine juice and stir again. Add balance of tangerine juice. Whisk well, then refrigerate 1 or 2 hours or until softly set.

5. Whisk the jelled tangerine mixture until it is broken up. Add ½ the reserved whipped cream and whisk together until smooth. Taste for sweetness and add 1 or 2 tablespoons powdered sugar if you like. Fold in the reserved tangerine pieces. Spoon into stem glasses, cover with plastic, and refrigerate.

6. Add 1 tablespoon powdered sugar to the remaining whipped cream. Reserve in refrigerator.

7. Peel 2 or 3 of the very small tangerines very carefully, keeping them whole. Slice tangerines across into ¼-inch-thick slices, then carefully remove any seeds with the point of a sharp knife. Place a tangerine slice, prettier side up, on top of each dessert. Pipe a rosette of whipped cream in the center of each tangerine slice.

TO SERVE: Serve chilled or bring out to room ½ hour before serving.

DO-AHEAD INFORMATION: The mousse may be prepared a day or two ahead and kept, covered with plastic, in the refrigerator. Tangerine slices and whipped cream decoration may be added 4 or 5 hours before serving.

TWO-LAYERED RASPBERRY MOUSSE
(serves 6)

With one deep red layer and one pink layer, this is undoubtedly one of the most beautiful desserts in the book. Yet its appeal goes beyond beauty because it captures the tart-sweet essence of raspberries. A final virtue is that you make it with frozen raspberries, which are affordable and always available.

INGREDIENTS:

1 cup whipping cream
3 10-ounce packages
    frozen red raspberries,
    packed with sugar
    and water, defrosted

2 tablespoons cold water
1 envelope plain gelatin
1 tablespoon powdered
    sugar

SERVING DISHES: 6 stem glasses

PROCEDURE:
1. Whip cream until stiff. Reserve in refrigerator.
2. Drain liquid from 1 package of raspberries, placing

raspberries on a plate and reserving syrup. Separate berries into 6 equal portions and reserve in refrigerator.

3. Drain juice from remaining 2 packages of raspberries, combining and reserving juices from all 3 packages. Choose 6 of the largest, prettiest raspberries and place on a plate and freeze for final decoration.

4. Have a medium-size strainer* with holes fine enough so that the raspberry seeds do not go through. Using a rubber spatula, push berries from 2 packages of raspberries through strainer, straining out and discarding seeds. Mix purée with all the raspberry juices and reserve. You will have about 2½ cups raspberry mixture.

5. Place cold water in a 4-cup glass beaker and sprinkle gelatin on top. Mix well, then let soften 1 minute. Microwave 30 seconds on high or heat in metal measuring cup over double boiler, then stir well, scraping bottom and sides of beaker with rubber spatula. Add ⅓ cup raspberry mixture and stir. Add balance and stir again.

6. Neatly pour a full ¼ cup of raspberry mixture into each serving glass. Add reserved whole raspberries (divided into sixths) from refrigerator, one portion to each glass.

7. Whisk half the reserved whipped cream with the balance of the raspberry mixture. Carefully pour equal portions of this mousse into the glasses so that the mixtures stay in separate layers. Refrigerate for 2 or more hours or until set, although if you're in a real hurry, this dessert is very nice only partially set.

TO SERVE: Whip balance of whipped cream stiff, adding powdered sugar. Pipe a rosette of cream on each dessert and place 1 frozen berry in center.

*This process can be tedious if you try to do it in a tiny strainer.

DO-AHEAD INFORMATION: Desserts may be prepared 1 or 2 days ahead. Cover each glass with plastic and keep refrigerated. Pipe on whipped-cream rosette 2 or 3 hours before serving and add frozen berry on the way to the table.

5

PIES, TARTS, AND CHEESECAKES

ALMOND CREAM PIE, ALMOND CRUST

BANANA CREAM PIE, MACAROON CRUST

CHOCOLATE PIE, WALNUT CHOCOLATE CRUST

MAGIC DEEP-DISH COCONUT CUSTARD PIE

LIZZY BURT'S STRAWBERRY-KIWI PAVLOVA

WALNUT PAVLOVA WITH PEACHES

PEANUT BUTTER CREAM PIE, CHOPPED PEANUT CRUST

NO-BAKE PUMPKIN PIE, MOLASSES PECAN CRUST

SOUR CREAM FRUIT PIE, COCONUT CRUST

STRAWBERRY PIE, ALMOND SHORTBREAD CRUST

MINCEMEAT TURNOVERS

MINI STRAWBERRY COOKIE TARTS

APRICOT-PINEAPPLE CHEESECAKE

NO-BAKE LEMON CHEESECAKE

RASPBERRY CHEESECAKE

This chapter contains an unusual combination of desserts. There are pies, three new, light cheesecakes, two meringue Pavlovas, a turnover, and some mini cookie tarts. The dishes are all easy and fast and they are all delicious.

The piecrusts in this chapter taste wonderful and are fun to do. They are mostly crumbled cookie crusts. There are a molasses cookie crust, an almond cookie crust, a coconut macaroon crust, a shortbread crust, and a lemon nut cookie crust. There are crusts made of nothing but chopped nuts or peanuts or coconut, sometimes with chocolate added. There are easy egg-white crusts, whole cookie "crusts" or pedestals, and even a bought puff-paste crust. In short, just about everything to make pies easier, and maybe even better tasting.

You will find a lot of Pepperidge Farm cookies used in this chapter. I am not getting paid for recommending them, but have chosen to use them because I like them, because they are free of unfamiliar additives, and because they are available almost everywhere. Feel free to substitute any cookie you like, especially an honest, good-tasting cookie from a local bakery. It's fun to experiment. You will probably come up with some better combinations than I have.

It's hard to name favorites in this chapter with such a mixture of different kinds of desserts, but here I go, anyway. In order of preference, I like the Chocolate Pie, Walnut Chocolate Crust; Sour Cream Fruit Pie, Coconut Crust; Banana Cream Pie, Macaroon Crust; Raspberry Cheesecake; No-Bake Lemon Cheesecake; and Mincemeat Turnovers.

WHIPPED-CREAM DECORATIONS

In the instructions for decorating the pies in this chapter you will frequently see: "Pipe swirls of sweetened, flavored whipped cream on top." Here are some specific piping suggestions:

Using a large pastry tip (Ateco 7-B or 8-B), pipe in a small circular motion 8 mounds of cream, 2 inches in diameter, around the top edge of the pie so that when the pie is cut into 8 pieces, each piece has its own decoration. You may add 1 or more of these in the center of the pie. It is nice to place something to identify the pie in these whipped-cream rosettes—a strawberry or strawberry slice, a raspberry, a black cherry, an almond, a banana slice, a few blueberries.

Make an overlapping coil design around the top outside edge and a few swirls or rosettes in the center, again adding some of the theme of the pie.

Make stripes, fat at the start and thinning toward the center, like spokes of a wheel radiating from the outer top edge to the center. Place a large rosette in the center and, if desired, more rosettes around the top edges.

Make rings of small rosettes, radiating from the center, allowing space in between so that the filling shows through.

MISCELLANEOUS PIE HINTS AND INFORMATION

To avoid crusts sticking to the bottom of a pie tin or dish, rub the tin or dish with ¼ teaspoon corn oil (or spray with nonstick spray) before adding the crust.

Ice cubes are added to some of the pie fillings in this chapter to cool the fillings so that they can be poured into the crusts right away. The 5 ice cubes specified in most of the recipes should equal ½ cup water. To check your ice cubes, place ½ cup water in a 1-cup measure, then add 5 cubes. Push the cubes down in the water, adding more, if necessary, so that the water level comes up to 1 cup. Pour out the water and you will have the correct amount of ice for the recipe.

Any of the pies using gelatin should be prepared at least 5 or 6 hours ahead to allow time to set properly. The pies may all be prepared a day ahead. The crusts stay amazingly crisp for 1 day, but start getting softer after that. Most of the pies and other desserts in this chapter do not freeze well, because of the fruits they contain; however, five of them freeze exceptionally well: the almond, chocolate, and peanut butter pies; the mincemeat turnovers; and the lemon cheesecake.

Just before cutting and serving the pies in this chapter, if baking in a tin, place the tin on the stove and heat just until it is slightly warm. This will melt the butter in the crust and free the bottom from the tin. If using a pie dish, warm the bottom of the dish in hot water, but not so hot as to crack the chilled dish.

ALMOND CREAM PIE, ALMOND CRUST
(serves 6 to 8)

This is a beautiful and delicious pie. It has an almond cookie crust and a ground almond pastry cream filling, and for a spectacular finish it can be topped with swirls of whipped cream and sprinkled with glazed, sliced almonds.

INGREDIENTS:

5 ounces almond cookies*
2¼ cups (11 ounces) almonds, unblanched or blanched (total)
½ stick (2 ounces) + 3 tablespoons unsalted butter (total)
2 tablespoons cold water
1 envelope plain gelatin

4 egg yolks
¾ cup sugar
2 tablespoons cornstarch
1½ cups milk
1 teaspoon vanilla
¼ teaspoon almond extract
5 ice cubes

SERVING DISH: A 9-inch pie tin or dish, lightly oiled

PROCEDURE:

1. Place cookies and 3 ounces (rounded ½ cup) almonds in container of food processor fitted with steel blade. Process 1 minute or to coarse crumbs. Melt ½ stick butter and

*Hard Italian-style almond cookies or almond macaroons are preferred (1 cup crumbs), but any cookie will do.

pour into crumbs. Process 5 seconds more, then dump crumbs into pie tin. Using fork and/or fingers, press onto bottom and sides to form a crust. Chill in freezer.

2. Mix water and gelatin in a small saucer. Reserve.

3. Whisk yolks and sugar in saucepan (heavy one preferred) just until mixed. Whisk in cornstarch. Add milk, then place over medium-high heat and bring to the boil, whisking constantly but casually. Lower heat and simmer for 3 minutes, whisking occasionally.

4. Transfer hot mixture to a bowl. Add 3 tablespoons butter plus gelatin, vanilla, and almond extract. Stir until butter has melted and gelatin has dissolved.

5. Place 8 ounces almonds in container of food processor fitted with steel blade. Process 1 minute or until well ground. Add ice cubes plus half the hot pudding mixture. Process for 30 seconds. Add balance of pudding mixture and process 2 or 3 seconds, no longer. Pour into chilled pie shell. Refrigerate until serving time.

TO SERVE: Serve chilled as is or pipe swirls of sweetened, flavored whipped cream (could flavor with Amaretto) and top with glazed, sliced almonds (see recipe for Grapes in Sherried Cream).

DO-AHEAD INFORMATION: Pie may be done 1 or 2 days ahead. Glazed almonds may be done weeks ahead. Cream may be prepared 8 hours ahead, but beat it again and pipe on pie 3 or 4 hours ahead or just before serving.

BANANA CREAM PIE, MACAROON CRUST
(serves 6 to 8)

The filling for this wonderful pie has gelatin in place of part of the traditional cornstarch thickening, making it seem lighter and more delicate. The easy coconut macaroon crust adds an unusual and delightful flavor. If, when serving this pie, you should have trouble with the crust sticking, warm the pan bottom for a few seconds over direct heat (if using a tin) or place in hot water. This slightly melts the butter and frees the crust.

INGREDIENTS:

8 ounces coconut
    macaroon cookies*
½ stick (2 ounces) + 3
    tablespoons unsalted
    butter (total)
2 tablespoons cold water
1 envelope plain gelatin
6 egg yolks

½ cup + 2 tablespoons
    sugar
3 tablespoons cornstarch
2 cups milk
2 teaspoons vanilla
5 ice cubes
3 ripe bananas

SERVING DISH: A 9-inch pie tin or dish, lightly oiled

PROCEDURE:

1. Place cookies in container of food processor fitted with steel blade. Process 1 minute, or to coarse crumbs. Melt ½ stick butter and pour onto crumbs. Process 5 seconds more, then dump in pie tin. Using a fork and/or fingers, press onto bottom and sides to form a crust. Chill 15 minutes in freezer.

*Hard, dry macaroons preferred (1½ cups crumbs).

2. Mix cold water and gelatin in a small saucer. Let soften 1 minute.

3. Whisk yolks and sugar in a saucepan (heavy one preferred) just until mixed. Whisk in cornstarch. Add milk, then place over medium-high heat and bring to the boil, whisking constantly but casually. Reduce heat to low and allow mixture to burp and bubble for 3 minutes, whisking occasionally. Transfer to a bowl. Add 3 tablespoons butter, cut into slices, gelatin mixture, and vanilla, then stir until butter has melted and gelatin has dissolved. Add ice cubes and stir until dissolved.

4. Measure out 1 cup of the filling mixture and place in freezer for 15 minutes or until partially set (filling will run over if you don't do this). Slice bananas and stir into pudding in bowl. Dump into chilled crust, leveling nicely, then refrigerate.

5. When reserved cup of pudding (and pie itself) has softly set, beat with a spatula until fairly smooth, then spread on top of pie. Reserve in refrigerator until serving time.

TO SERVE: Serve chilled, as is, or pipe sweetened, flavored whipped cream on top and decorate at the last minute with a few banana slices.

DO-AHEAD INFORMATION: Crust may be prepared 2 or more days ahead. Pie may be filled 1 day ahead. Cream for decorating may be prepared 8 hours ahead, but beat again and pipe on 3 or 4 hours ahead or just before serving.

CHOCOLATE PIE, WALNUT CHOCOLATE CRUST
(serves 6 to 8)

The briefest-stay-as-a-leftover-in-the-refrigerator award was won by this dessert, hands down. My taster friends are still talking about this wonderful chocolate pie. The crust is nutty, crunchy, chocolatey, and wonderful. The filling is dark, smooth, and chocolatey, and wonderful. You're going to love this.

INGREDIENTS:

8 ounces walnuts (2½ cups)

2 ounces semisweet chocolate*

2 tablespoons unsalted butter

1 cup + 1 tablespoon sugar (total)

2 tablespoons cold water

1 envelope plain gelatin

2 ounces unsweetened chocolate

1 cup whipping cream

½ cup milk

6 egg yolks

1 teaspoon vanilla

5 ice cubes (½ cup frozen water)

SERVING DISH: A 9-inch pie dish, lightly oiled

PROCEDURE:

1. Place walnuts in container of food processor fitted with steel blade. Process until chopped coarse, about ⅛-inch dice. Reserve in processor.

2. Place semisweet chocolate, butter, and 2 tablespoons sugar in a 1-quart glass beaker and microwave 1½ minutes on high or until melted. Stir, then add to walnuts in processor. Process 3 seconds, then add 1 tablespoon sugar, stir, and

*I used Nestlé's real semisweet chocolate morsels (⅓ cup + 1 tablespoon).

process another 2 seconds. (This sugar is supposed to crunch.) Dump in pie tin or dish and, using a fork, and/or fingers, press onto bottom and sides to form a crust. Reserve in refrigerator.

3. Mix cold water and gelatin in a small saucer. Reserve.

4. Chop the unsweetened chocolate into coarse pieces and reserve in a bowl.

5. Have ready on the side a clean bowl and a rubber spatula. Place cream, milk, yolks, and remaining 1 cup minus 2 tablespoons sugar in a saucepan (preferably heavy). Over medium heat, whisking occasionally, bring just to the *first signs* of a boil (3 to 5 minutes). Immediately pour mixture into clean bowl. With rubber spatula, scrape any curdled part from the bottom of the pan, adding it to mixture. Whisk in vanilla. Right away, add softened gelatin and whisk to dissolve.

6. Immediately add ½ cup of the hot vanilla custard to the chopped chocolate and whisk until chocolate melts. Dump the chocolate mixture back into the balance of the hot custard. Whisk until smooth. Add ice cubes and stir until melted. Pour into prepared crust. Refrigerate until serving time.

TO SERVE: Serve chilled, as is, or to make it more beautiful, pipe swirls of sweetened, flavored whipped cream on top and sprinkle chocolate curls (See Grapes in Rum Butterscotch Cream) over the cream.

DO-AHEAD INFORMATION: Crust may be prepared 2 or 3 days ahead. Fill pie the day you are going to eat it, as crust softens after a day or so in the refrigerator. Whip cream and decorate pie 4 or 5 hours before serving. Keep refrigerated and do not keep more than 3 or 4 days.

MAGIC DEEP-DISH COCONUT CUSTARD PIE
(serves 6 to 8)

This square, deep-dish pie is delicious and wholesome as
well as magic. The recipe is an odd one that has been around
for years. An Australian friend sent me a similar one not
long ago; so you see, it has gotten around and even Down
Under. The magic of the recipe is that it appears to be
crustless, yet after baking, ta-da! a crust magically appears.
The explanation for this (sorry to ruin the illusion) is that,
in the early stages of baking, the thin custard cannot hold
the butter and flour in solution so they filter down and cook
as a separate layer.

INGREDIENTS:

¾ cup sugar (or less)
½ cup all-purpose flour
5 eggs, room temperature
3 cups milk, room
    temperature
½ stick (2 ounces)
    unsalted butter,
    melted

2 teaspoons vanilla
½ teaspoon nutmeg
1½ cups (3 ounces)
    shredded coconut,
    lightly packed; could
    use less

COOKING UTENSIL: An 8 × 8 × 2-inch ovenproof baking
dish

PROCEDURE:

   1. Preheat oven to 350 degrees.
   2. In container of food processor, fitted with steel blade,
place all the ingredients except the coconut, in the order
listed. Process 2 seconds.

3. Add 1 cup coconut and process 2 seconds, then pour into baking dish.

4. Sprinkle balance of coconut over top.

5. Bake in 350-degree oven 35 to 40 minutes, or until custard is puffed up and top is slightly browned. Do not overbake.

6. Allow to cool on rack. As it cools, push down from time to time on top outer edges to help keep pie level as it shrinks.

TO SERVE: Serve slightly warm, room temperature, or chilled, cut into squares, as is.

DO-AHEAD INFORMATION: May be done 1 or 2 days ahead. Keep refrigerated, as it is perishable.

LIZZY BURT'S STRAWBERRY-KIWI PAVLOVA
(serves 6 to 8)

Lizzy Burt, cooking teacher and friend, is a former Australian currently living in Ann Arbor, Michigan. This is my version of her version of a popular Australian meringue dessert. It consists of a meringue crown with a very fragile outer crust, an air space, then an inside soft center. There is a hollow in the center which is later filled and decorated with whipped cream and fruits.

In case you're wondering, the dessert, a kind of beautiful but simplified version of a Spanish Wind Torte, was named for Anna Pavlova, the noted ballerina, upon the occasion of a series of performances in Australia in the 1920s.

INGREDIENTS:

3 egg whites

¾ cup + 1–2 tablespoons granulated sugar (total)

1 teaspoon cornstarch

1 teaspoon vanilla

1 teaspoon vinegar

3 tablespoons water

1 cup whipping cream

1–2 tablespoons powdered sugar (optional)

2 pints strawberries

2 kiwis*

Mint leaves (optional)

COOKING UTENSIL AND SERVING DISH: A baking sheet plus a pretty plate or silver platter for serving

PROCEDURE:

1. Preheat oven to 250 degrees.

2. Butter a baking sheet in 4 spots, then press a 10-inch square of aluminum foil on top. Butter and flour the foil. Trace an 8-inch circle to use as a guide. Reserve.

3. Place egg whites, ¾ cup granulated sugar, cornstarch, vanilla, vinegar, and water in a bowl (not too large), then beat with an electric mixer for 5 minutes or until meringue is stiff enough to stay in the bowl when turned upside down.

4. Spoon 8 mounds of meringue onto the foil in a ring just inside the guide circle, then place the last of the me-

*Many other fruit combinations may be used for this. One popular one is passion fruit and strawberries. Squeeze passion fruit juice over the whipped cream and distribute seeds over, then add strawberries. You might also use fresh raspberries or even semidefrosted frozen ones, but add these at the very last minute.

ringue in the center and smooth it down to make the floor of the pie.

5. Bake in preheated 250-degree oven 1½ hours, then turn off oven and leave meringue in for 30 minutes more. Remove from oven, then carefully lift from the sheet and peel foil off bottom of meringue. Place meringue base on rack and let cool 15 minutes. Wrap well in plastic and store in room until serving time.

6. Whip cream and powdered sugar until stiff. Reserve in refrigerator until serving time. Brush strawberries with a damp towel (or at the last possible moment, wash and dry very well), then hull. Keep some pretty ones whole for decoration, then slice balance, sprinkle lightly with 1–2 tablespoons granulated sugar, and reserve (optional: crush ¼ and pass around as a sauce at the table). Peel kiwis and reserve.

7. Assemble 2 or 3 hours before serving. Whip cream stiff (add powdered sugar, if using), then spread over center area of meringue shell. Arrange some whole berries in clusters on the platter around the edge of the meringue. Place sliced strawberries and kiwis over whipped cream in center, placing mint leaves here and there. Reserve in refrigerator until serving time.

TO SERVE: Serve chilled.

DO-AHEAD INFORMATION: The meringue shell may be done 1 or 2 days ahead. Store it in the room, lightly covered with waxed paper. Strawberries may be hulled, sliced, and sugared 4 or 5 hours ahead and the whole thing assembled 2 or 3 hours before serving.

WALNUT PAVLOVA WITH PEACHES
(serves 6 to 8)

This is a delicious variation of Lizzy Burt's Pavlova. Chopped walnuts are added to the meringue and the shell is served with fresh peaches and shaved chocolate instead of strawberries and kiwis. The nut Pavlova flattens a little in baking and doesn't look quite so glamorous as the one without nuts, but it tastes so good, you won't mind.

INGREDIENTS:

3 egg whites
¾ cup + 1–2 tablespoons granulated sugar (total)
1 teaspoon cornstarch
2 teaspoons vanilla (total)
1 teaspoon vinegar
3 tablespoons water

1 cup (4 ounces) ground walnuts*
1½ pounds peaches†
2 cups whipping cream
4 tablespoons powdered sugar
⅓ cup (2 ounces) real semisweet chocolate morsels

COOKING UTENSIL AND SERVING DISH: A baking sheet plus a pretty plate or silver platter for serving.

PROCEDURE:

1. Preheat oven to 250 degrees.
2. Butter a baking sheet in 4 spots, then press a 10-inch

*Walnuts may be chopped in the food processor or ground in a grinder. You may use ½ walnuts and ½ hazelnuts for this for an unusual taste, or all almonds.
†Canned peaches or pears may be used for this, or fresh strawberries, or fresh or canned mangoes.

square of aluminum foil on top. Butter and flour the foil. Trace an 8-inch circle to use as a guide. Reserve.

3. Place egg whites, ¾ cup granulated sugar, cornstarch, 1 teaspoon vanilla, vinegar, and water in a bowl; then, using a hand-held electric mixer, beat at top speed for 5 or 6 minutes, or until meringue is stiff enough to stay in bowl when inverted. Dump nuts on top and fold in, using fewest possible strokes.

4. Spoon 8 mounds of meringue in a ring onto the foil just inside the guide circle, then place the last of the meringue in the center and smooth it down to make the floor of the pie.

5. Bake 2½ hours at 250 degrees, then turn off oven and leave meringue in oven 1 hour more. Carefully lift from baking sheet and peel foil off bottom of meringue. Place meringue on rack and let cool 15 minutes. Cover with sheet of waxed paper or wrap air-tight in plastic and store in room.

6. Peel peaches, cut into bite-size pieces, and place in a bowl. Sprinkle with 1 or 2 tablespoons sugar. Place cream, powdered sugar, and 1 teaspoon vanilla in another bowl and whip until stiff. Reserve cream and peaches separately in refrigerator.

7. Two or 3 hours before serving, assemble the dessert. Reserve some peach pieces for final decoration, then give the cream a final beat to stiffen and add half to the peaches, reserving other half of cream for final decoration. Stir peaches in cream, then place in center area of Pavlova. Reserve in refrigerator until serving time.

TO SERVE: Pipe swirls of whipped cream on top. Place peach pieces here and there, then chop chocolate bits a little smaller and sprinkle around. Serve.

DO-AHEAD INFORMATION: Meringue may be made 1 or 2 days ahead. Slice peaches and whip the cream 5 or 6 hours before serving. Final assembly may be done 2 or 3 hours before serving, but no sooner than that as the meringue will get too soggy. Final decoration could be done at that time also, but add peach pieces at last minute as they will turn dark.

PEANUT BUTTER CREAM PIE, CHOPPED PEANUT CRUST
(serves 6 to 8)

This is a delightful pie featuring a chopped peanut crust and a creamy-smooth peanut filling. My best friends looked at me kind of funny when I told them about my Peanut Butter Pie, but they ate it and loved it.

INGREDIENTS:
6½ ounces peanuts*
⅔ cup sugar + 2 tablespoons sugar (total)
2 tablespoons unsalted butter
1 cup + 2 tablespoons

(9 ounces) creamy peanut butter (preferably unsalted)
2 cups milk (total)
2 envelopes plain gelatin
1 teaspoon vanilla
5 ice cubes

SERVING DISH: A 9-inch pie tin or dish, lightly oiled

*Planters cocktail peanuts or red-skin Spanish peanuts both work fine for this.

PROCEDURE:

1. Rinse and dry peanuts (if salted), then place in container of food processor fitted with steel blade. Pulse on and off until nuts are chopped coarsely. Add 2 tablespoons sugar and process with 2 quick pulses. Melt and add butter and process with 4 or 5 quick pulses. Dump into pie tin, then press down to line bottom and sides using fork and/or wet fingers. Refrigerate.

2. Place peanut butter in food processor fitted with steel blade. Reserve.

3. Mix ½ cup milk plus gelatin in a 1-quart glass beaker and let soften 1 minute. Microwave 1½ minutes on high power or until boiling hot. Add ⅔ cup sugar, 1½ cups milk, and vanilla. Stir to dissolve sugar, then add to peanut butter in processor and process until mixed. Add ice cubes and process until dissolved. Pour into prepared crust. Refrigerate until serving time.

TO SERVE: Serve chilled, as is, or pipe swirls of sweetened, flavored whipped cream on top. For an extra touch, sprinkle chopped, toasted peanuts, rinsed of any salt, over the cream.

DO-AHEAD INFORMATION: Pie and filling may be done 1 or 2 days ahead. Whipped cream may be prepared 8 hours ahead, but beat it again and pipe on pie 3 or 4 hours ahead or just before serving.

NO-BAKE PUMPKIN PIE, MOLASSES PECAN CRUST
(serves 6 to 8)

The distinguishing feature of this pumpkin pie, other than the fact that you don't have to bake it, is its delightful, crisp molasses-cookie, chopped pecan crust. This is a delicious pumpkin pie and an easy one.

INGREDIENTS:

5¾ ounces Molasses
    Crisps*
½ cup (1¾ ounces)
    pecans
½ stick (2 ounces)
    unsalted butter
¼ cup milk
2 envelopes plain gelatin

6 eggs
2 16-ounce cans
    solid-pack pumpkin†
½ cup sugar
1½ teaspoons cinnamon
1 teaspoon ground ginger
¼ teaspoon ground cloves
¼ cup dark molasses

SERVING DISH: A 9-inch pie tin or dish, lightly oiled

PROCEDURE:

1. Place cookies and pecans in container of food processor fitted with steel blade. Process 20–30 seconds, or to coarse crumbs. Melt butter and add to crumbs. Process 5 seconds, then dump into pie tin. Using fork and/or fingers, press onto bottom and sides to form a crust. Chill in refrigerator.

2. Mix milk with gelatin and reserve.

3. Warm eggs by placing them, in their shells, in a bowl and covering them with hot water. Let sit 5 minutes.

4. Place pumpkin, sugar, spices, and molasses in a saucepan (heavy one preferred) and bring to a complete boil, stirring occasionally. Add softened gelatin and whisk to dissolve. Add warmed eggs and whisk to thoroughly mix. Pour into a bowl and let cool 30 minutes. Place in freezer for

*These are Pepperidge Farm cookies. You may substitute gingersnaps (1½ cups crumbs), but taste after grinding with nuts and add 1 tablespoon sugar if desired.
†I used Libby's.

1 hour (stir halfway through), then stir again and pour into chilled pie shell. Reserve in refrigerator until serving time.

TO SERVE: Serve chilled, as is, or with ice cream on the side, and/or swirls of sweetened, flavored whipped cream piped on top.

DO-AHEAD INFORMATION: Crust may be done 4 or 5 days ahead; pie may be filled 1 day ahead. Whipped cream may be prepared 8 hours ahead, but beat again and pipe on pie 3 or 4 hours ahead or just before serving. This pie is perishable. Keep refrigerated.

SOUR CREAM FRUIT PIE, COCONUT CRUST
(serves 6 to 8)

This pie, fit for the gods, is based on that old dessert, ambrosia. You may call it Ambrosia Pie, if you don't think that's too tacky. If you can't find sweet, yellowish-white seedless grapes (don't buy the tart green ones), increase the quantities of the oranges and bananas, and leave the grapes out.

INGREDIENTS:

2 cups (4 ounces) sweetened flake-style or shredded coconut

½ stick (2 ounces) unsalted butter, room temperature

1 cup milk (total)

1 envelope plain gelatin

3–4 tablespoons sugar

1 8¾-ounce tin apricot halves

8 ounces sour cream

1½ cups (7 ounces) seedless white grapes

3 oranges (1½ cups sliced)

1 large banana (1 cup diced)

SERVING DISH: A 9-inch pie tin or dish

PROCEDURE:

1. Stir coconut and butter in a bowl, then dump into pie tin or dish. Press down with fork and/or fingers to line bottom and sides. Chill 15 minutes in freezer.

2. Place ½ cup milk in a 1-quart glass beaker. Add gelatin and stir, then let soften 1 minute. Microwave 1½ minutes on high or melt in saucepan. Add sugar, then whisk to dissolve. Add balance of ½ cup milk plus drained apricots (6 halves), chopped fine, plus sour cream. Whisk until well mixed, then place in freezer for 15 minutes or until starting to set.

3. Stem, then wash and dry grapes. Cut rind and membrane from oranges. Cut into quarters lengthwise, then cut across into ¼-inch slices. Set aside 8 or 10 attractive pieces to use as decoration at the end. Dice bananas. There should be a total of 4 cups of the 3 fruits.

4. Stir sour cream mixture, then add fruits and mix well. Dump into pie shell; refrigerate until serving time.

TO SERVE: Serve chilled, as is, or decorate with sweetened, flavored whipped cream, arranging reserved orange slices on top.

DO-AHEAD INFORMATION: May be done 1 or 2 days ahead. Cover with plastic; keep refrigerated.

STRAWBERRY PIE, ALMOND SHORTBREAD CRUST
(serves 6 to 8)

Although it looks like a pie, is served in a pie tin, and is called a pie, this dessert is really a tart. Whole strawberries are placed standing up in an almond shortbread cookie crust, then covered up to their necks with sweetened crushed strawberries thickened with gelatin. Whether you call it a tart or a pie or George, it is a lovely, refreshing, and delicious dessert.

I am so thoroughly depressed by the lack of sweetness and flavor in California strawberries these days that I recommend your doing this pie only if you can find good local berries.

INGREDIENTS:

1 5½-ounce package shortbread cookies*
⅔ cup (3 ounces) almonds
1–3 (or more) tablespoons sugar (total)
½ stick (2 ounces) unsalted butter

2 pints fresh strawberries
1 10-ounce package frozen, sliced strawberries,† with sugar, defrosted
2 tablespoons cold water
1 envelope plain gelatin

COOKING UTENSIL AND SERVING DISH: A 9-inch baking tin or dish, lightly oiled

PROCEDURE:

1. Preheat oven to 350 degrees.

2. Place cookies, almonds, and 1 tablespoon sugar in container of food processor fitted with steel blade (or grind

*I used Pepperidge Farm.
†I used Flav-R-Pac frozen strawberries from Portland, Oregon.

through a grinder) and process 20 seconds, or to coarse crumbs. Melt butter, then add and process 5 seconds. Dump into pie tin.

3. Using fork and/or fingers, press crumbs on bottom and sides of tin. Bake in preheated 350-degree oven for 10 minutes. Let cool 10 minutes on a rack, then place in freezer for 30 minutes to chill.

4. Brush (or wash and dry well) and hull fresh strawberries. Set aside 4 or 5 to be cut in half and used for decoration. Pick out enough of the next best and ripest to stand up in the bottom of the tin and set them aside. Place balance of berries in food processor and add defrosted frozen strawberries and syrup. Process to a coarse purée. Add 1–2 tablespoons sugar or more, as desired, and stir to dissolve. Reserve.

5. Place cold water and gelatin in a 1-quart glass beaker, then stir to mix. Let soften 1 minute, then microwave 45 seconds on high or melt in saucepan until mixture is boiling hot. Whisk into strawberry mixture. Reserve in room until ready to use.

6. When crust is properly chilled, stand reserved strawberries in bottom of pie shell. Stir strawberry purée, then pour over berries in crust. Refrigerate until serving time.

TO SERVE: Pipe sweetened, flavored whipped cream on edges and in center, then place reserved strawberry halves on top. Serve.

DO-AHEAD INFORMATION: Pie may be prepared 1 day ahead. Whipped-cream topping may be prepared 8 hours ahead, but should be beaten again and piped on no more than 3 to 4 hours before serving.

MINCEMEAT TURNOVERS
(makes 6 small turnovers)

These lovely turnovers are a variation of English Eccles cakes. You wouldn't normally expect to find a complicated pastry such as this in a cookbook of simple recipes; however, with packaged mincemeat and ready-to-roll puff-paste sheets available almost everywhere today, turnovers easily fit into the simple category.

INGREDIENTS:

1 17¼-ounce package Pepperidge Farm frozen puff pastry, defrosted

1 9-ounce box condensed mincemeat*
½ cup water
1 egg, beaten
1½ teaspoons sugar

PROCEDURE:

1. Remove 1 9½-inch puff-paste sheet from package (return other sheet to freezer to use another day). Unfold and let sit 20 minutes.

2. Crumble mincemeat and place in saucepan with water. Bring to a boil, then boil 1 minute. Spread on a dinner plate and place in freezer for 30 minutes or until chilled.

3. Preheat oven to 400 degrees.

4. Roll puff-paste sheet, flouring well, to 12 × 18 inches. Trim to an even rectangle, then cut into 6 6-inch squares. Don't be too fussy. Cut corners from squares, cutting in about 1 inch.

4. Divide mincemeat into 6 portions, a scant ¼ cup each. Place 1 portion in center of each dough square. Flatten filling to a disk, 3 inches in diameter.

*I used Borden's.

5. You are going to make round cakes by covering the filling with the dough. Start by folding one section of the dough to the center. Brush that piece with beaten egg, which acts as glue, then fold over the next little area, sticking it down to the egg-brushed area, and making similar folds and tucks as you go. Continue until you have come around and the filling is completely covered.

6. Place cakes on a baking sheet with the folds underneath. Brush tops of cakes with beaten egg, then sprinkle ¼ teaspoon sugar over each. Cut 2 or 3 slits in the top of each cake.

7. Bake in top third of 400-degree oven for 25 minutes, or until nicely browned.

TO SERVE: Serve hot or room temperature (with vanilla ice cream, if you like). To reheat, bake 10 to 15 minutes in 300-degree oven.

DO-AHEAD INFORMATION: The turnovers could be assembled a day ahead (or frozen and kept longer), then baked (defrosted) on serving day.

MINI STRAWBERRY COOKIE TARTS
(makes 12)

These are the prettiest little things you ever saw, yet they are incredibly easy to do. When you are finished they will look so professional, nobody will believe you made them. Strawberries are placed on small cookies, then painted with melted red jelly. Later, tiny whipped-cream decorations are piped around the base. The piping is the only problem and if you get the right tip and just plunge in, you'll be surprised at how easy it is.

After trying many cookies as bases for these little tarts, I liked the Orleans sandwich cookies the best. The thin chocolate coating between the two cookies may seem a little vulgar, but I think you'll be able to stand it.

INGREDIENTS:

10 Pepperidge Farm
   Orleans sandwich
   cookies*
1 pint fresh, ripe
   strawberries

2 tablespoons red currant
   jelly†
½ cup whipping cream
1 tablespoon powdered
   sugar

PROCEDURE:

1. Place cookies on a serving dish. Wipe berries with a damp cloth (or wash and dry well), then cut slices from the large ends, which will hull berries and flatten their bottoms at the same time.

2. Heat jelly to boiling in a small saucepan, then brush over the tops of the cookies. Place 1 large strawberry in the center of each cookie, then brush each berry with the hot jelly. Chill in refrigerator.

3. Place cream and powdered sugar in a small bowl and whip until stiff enough to pipe. Place in pastry bag fitted with small, decorative tip (Ateco #0 or 0-B), then pipe tiny whipped-cream rosettes around the base of each strawberry. Refrigerate until serving time.

*These come in 5¼-ounce packages containing 15 cookies. If you want to do them all, you will probably need 2 pints of strawberries. Any 2-inch-round cookie will do for these. If cookie is rounded on top, scrape with a knife to flatten and brush with jelly, then stick strawberry on.

†You could substitute raspberry jelly or any red jelly for this.

TO SERVE: Serve chilled as is. These are meant to be picked up with fingers and eaten. Serve them to accompany a simple ice-cream dessert.

DO-AHEAD INFORMATION: The mini tarts, except for the whipped-cream decoration, may be prepared 8 to 10 hours ahead (or even a day ahead, but remember that the strawberries go on ripening). You may prepare the whipped cream 8 hours ahead, but beat it again and pipe on 5 or 6 hours before serving. *Leave tarts uncovered in refrigerator. This is important. If you store them air-tight, the jam coating softens and runs off.*

APRICOT-PINEAPPLE CHEESECAKE
(serves 6 to 8)

This delicious and different cheesecake features, in its supporting cast, a combination of puréed fruit and fruit juices in place of the usual milk or cream. The apricot and pineapple add zest and a lovely apricot color to this very delightful dessert.

INGREDIENTS:

5½ ounces Lemon Nut Crunch cookies* (1⅓ cups crumbs)

½ cup almonds (2 ounces)

½ stick (2 ounces) unsalted butter

8 ounces cream cheese

1 29-ounce can apricots (unpeeled halves)

*I used Pepperidge Farm Lemon Nut Crunch cookies, but any cookie will do.

1 8-ounce can crushed (or
   chunk) pineapple in
   unsweetened
   pineapple juice
2 tablespoons cold water

1 envelope plain gelatin
¼ cup sugar (or more)
9 glacéed cherries*
   (optional)

SERVING DISH: A 9-inch pie tin or dish, lightly oiled

PROCEDURE:

1. Place cookies and almonds in container of food processor fitted with steel blade (or grind through grinder) and process to coarse crumbs. Melt butter, then add and process 5 seconds. Dump crumbs into pie tin. Using fork and/or fingers, press on bottom and sides of tin to form a crust. Place in freezer to chill.

2. Place cream cheese in container of food processor fitted with steel blade. Process 5 seconds or until smooth. Reserve.

3. Drain syrup from apricots and reserve for another use. Set aside 9 small apricot halves to use for decoration later. Add balance of apricots to cream cheese in processor and process to a purée, coarse or smooth as you like. Reserve in processor.

4. Place crushed pineapple (chop, if using chunks) and liquid in a small saucepan. Bring to a boil, then simmer 2 minutes. Strain, spreading pineapple on a plate and returning juice (about ⅓ cup) to saucepan.

5. Stir cold water and gelatin in a cup, then let sit 1 minute to soften. Return pineapple juice to the boil. Off heat, add softened gelatin and stir to dissolve, then add sugar and stir to dissolve. Add to mixture in processor, then

*These may be marinated in rum for a few hours if you like. You may substitute maraschino cherries.

process to mix. Stir in crushed pineapple. Pour into prepared pie shell. Reserve in refrigerator until serving time.

TO SERVE: Arrange 8 apricot halves, holes up, around outer top edges of pie and 1 in the center, then place cherries in apricot depressions. Serve.

DO-AHEAD INFORMATION: Crust may be prepared 3 or 4 days ahead. Pie may be filled 1 or 2 days ahead. Add decorations 5 or 6 hours before serving.

NO-BAKE LEMON CHEESECAKE
(serves 6 to 8)

This is a cheesecake pie made of a wonderful, crunchy cookie-almond crust and a marvelous jellied cheesecake filling. This truly delicious pie is a favorite of mine.

INGREDIENTS:

5½ ounces Lemon Nut Crunch cookies* (1⅓ cups crumbs)
½ cup (2 ounces) almonds
½ stick (2 ounces) unsalted butter

8 ounces cream cheese
2 cups milk (total)
Grated zest of 1 lemon
¼ cup lemon juice
1 envelope plain gelatin
½ cup sugar

SERVING DISH: A 9-inch pie tin or dish, lightly oiled

*I used Pepperidge Farm Lemon Nut Crunch cookies, but any cookie will do.

PROCEDURE:

1. Place cookies and almonds in container of food processor fitted with steel blade (or grind through grinder) and process to coarse crumbs. Melt butter, then add to crumbs and process 5 seconds more. Dump crumbs into pie tin. Using fork and/or fingers, press on bottom and sides of tin to form a crust. Place in freezer to chill.

2. Place cream cheese in container of food processor fitted with steel blade. Process 5 seconds, or until free of lumps. Add 1½ cups milk slowly, first adding ¼ cup, processing, stirring bottom and sides, then adding another ¼ cup, processing and stirring. Add remaining cup all at once along with the lemon zest and juice. Process until smooth. Reserve in processor.

3. Whisk ½ cup milk plus gelatin in a 1-quart glass beaker. Let soften 1 minute, then microwave 1½ minutes on high power or melt in saucepan. Add sugar and whisk to dissolve. Turn on food processor and pour hot gelatin mixture down feed tube. Dump into a bowl and place in freezer for 15 minutes.

4. Whisk partially set cheesecake mixture until smooth, then pour into prepared pie shell. Refrigerate until serving time.

TO SERVE: Serve chilled, as is. To make this more festive, pipe swirls of sweetened, flavored (lemon would be good) whipped cream on top. Cut thin lemon slices in fourths and place here and there on the cream.

DO-AHEAD INFORMATION: Crust may be prepared 3 or 4 days ahead. Pie may be filled 1 or 2 days ahead. Optional whipped-cream topping may be prepared 8 hours ahead, but beat again and pipe on 3 or 4 hours ahead or just before serving.

RASPBERRY CHEESECAKE
(serves 8)

This is an elegant and delicious pie. The raspberries give it a gorgeous color and a wonderful flavor and texture. The unusual combination of the raspberry filling with the molasses cookie crust is immensely appealing to me, but if you find the molasses taste too down-on-the-farm, use a light lemon cookie instead.

INGREDIENTS:

5¾ ounces Molasses
    Crisps*
½ stick (2 ounces)
    unsalted butter
2 10-ounce packages
    frozen raspberries,
packed with sugar
    and water
16 ounces cream cheese
½ cup + 2 tablespoons
    milk (total)
1 envelope plain gelatin
1 teaspoon vanilla

SERVING DISH: A 9-inch pie tin or dish, lightly oiled

PROCEDURE:

1. Place cookies in container of food processor fitted with steel blade. Process 15 seconds or to coarse crumbs. Melt butter, then add and process 5 seconds. Dump into pie

*These are Pepperidge Farm cookies. You may substitute 1½ cups gingersnap crumbs or mild lemon cookie crumbs if you prefer.

tin. Using fork and/or fingers, press onto bottom and sides to form a crust. Chill in freezer.

2. Have raspberries defrosted, but keep packages separate. Dump contents of first package into a strainer over a bowl, then strain and discard seeds. Reserve. Strain syrup from second package of raspberries, reserving whole raspberries and syrup separately.

3. Break cream cheese into smaller pieces and place into container of food processor fitted with steel blade. Process and stir until lump-free. Add raspberry syrup-purée from first package, then process, stirring as necessary, until smooth. Reserve in processor.

4. Place ¼ cup milk in a glass beaker. Add gelatin, then stir and let soften 1 minute. Microwave 30 seconds or until boiling hot. Whisk to mix, then add to cream cheese mixture in processor and process until blended. Add ¼ cup milk plus 2 tablespoons (or more, to taste) reserved syrup from second raspberry package, plus vanilla. Process to blend. Pour mixture into prepared pie shell. Place reserved whole raspberries over filling, adding them one by one and distributing well (optional: using a fork, cover berries with filling). Refrigerate until serving time.

TO SERVE: Serve as is or pipe swirls of sweetened, flavored whipped cream on top.

DO-AHEAD INFORMATION: Crust may be done 4 or 5 days ahead; pie may be filled 1 day ahead. Whipped cream may be prepared 8 hours ahead, but beat again and pipe on pie 3 or 4 hours ahead or just before serving.

6

CAKES, SIMPLE AND FANCY

GROUND ALMOND CAKE

CHUNKY SPICED APPLE CAKE

APPLE PECAN CAKE

BLACKBERRY KUCHEN

BROWN SUGAR PECAN SQUARES

LIGHT CARROT ALMOND CAKE

CHOCOLATE BABA CAKE

QUEEN OF SHEBA CHOCOLATE SQUARES

CHOCOLATE SAUCE CAKE

CHOCOLATE SYRUP BUNDT CAKE WITH GRAND MARNIER

NANA'S GINGERBREAD

ORANGE LIQUEUR CAKE WITH WALNUTS AND RAISINS

PINEAPPLE PECAN UPSIDE-DOWN CAKE

FILLED POPPY-SEED CAKE

This chapter is another of those with an amazing variety of different-style desserts. The cakes in this group range from very proper tea cakes to chunk-style cakes with fruits; from dark, rich, frosted chocolate squares to moist, light chocolate whipped-cream cake squares; and from Nana's dense, old-fashioned gingerbread to the best Pineapple Upside-Down Cake you ever ate in your life. You are in for a great variety of wonderful treats.

I do not pretend to have created most of the cakes in this chapter. In general, they are traditional cakes that homemakers have been baking for years. Home cooks were making Spiced Apple Cake, Brown Sugar Pecan Squares, Chocolate Sauce Cake, Pineapple Upside-Down Cake, and Blackberry Kuchen long before any of us was born. I have worked on these cakes, however, and come up with my versions of them. In some cases they are quite different from the traditional versions. In other cases, I tried and tried to make my imprint, but they resisted and I ended up using them pretty much as they were.

Here are my top seven favorite cakes in this chapter in the *reverse* order of preference: Brown Sugar Pecan Squares,

Nana's Gingerbread, Apple Pecan Cake, Chunky Spiced Apple Cake, Blackberry Kuchen, Chocolate Baba Cake, and (ta-da) Pineapple Pecan Upside-Down Cake.

SOME SPECIAL CAKE-MAKING HINTS
FOR THIS CHAPTER

Some of the cakes in the chapter call for an 8 × 8-inch tin and some call for the same-size baking dish. I like using the dish because you can see the bottom of the cake as it's cooking, but I frequently use the tin, because it has a slightly smaller capacity, which is better for the quantities of certain cakes.

On warming eggs: I have found that some cakes bake to more even, level layers if all the ingredients used are room temperature or warmer. That is why, in certain recipes, the eggs and the milk are warmed.

In any recipe where you see instructions to put eggs and sugar in a bowl together, make sure to mix the eggs and sugar right away. If sugar is dumped on top of an egg yolk and allowed to sit (while you go answer the phone or stop to chat with the mailman), the sugar causes the yolk to form a hard crust that will not dissolve when you beat the eggs later.

GROUND ALMOND CAKE
(serves 6)

I discovered this cake in 1969 as a student at the Cordon Bleu in Paris. It was called *pain de Gênes,* or Genoa bread, indicating a probable Italian origin. The cake is wholesome and simple, the kind that people in the old days would sprinkle with powdered sugar and serve at teatime. It works fine in today's world, served as a dessert with whipped cream, ice cream, or a Vanilla English Cream sauce. It has an old-fashioned taste and is dense, moist, nutty, and delicious.

INGREDIENTS:

3 eggs

⅔ cup (3 ounces) unblanched almonds

⅔ cup all-purpose flour

1 stick (4 ounces) unsalted butter

¾ cup granulated sugar

1 tablespoon orange liqueur

1 teaspoon vanilla

Powdered sugar

COOKING UTENSIL: An 8 × 8 × 2-inch baking tin, buttered and floured

PROCEDURE:

1. Preheat oven to 350 degrees. Warm eggs by placing them, in their shells, in a bowl and covering them with hot water. Let sit 5 minutes.

2. Place almonds and flour in container of food processor fitted with steel blade. Process 1 minute or until nuts are ground fine. Reserve.

3. Slice butter and place in a 1-quart glass beaker. Mi-

crowave 30 to 60 seconds, then beat a few seconds with a hand-held electric mixer until fluffy and smooth. Add sugar and beat 2 minutes. Add eggs, 1 at a time, beating 1 minute after adding each. Fold in almond-flour mixture. Add orange liqueur and vanilla. Dump into prepared cake tin and spread to level.

4. Bake in preheated 350-degree oven 40 minutes, or until medium-brown and done. Let cool in tin 5 minutes, then turn out on a rack and allow to cool. Store air-tight in room. This cake seems to get better the second or third day.

TO SERVE: Sprinkle with powdered sugar, then cut into squares and serve as is or with ice cream, sweetened, flavored whipped cream, or Vanilla English Cream.

DO-AHEAD INFORMATION: The cake keeps for a week air-tight in the room. Freeze it if you wish to keep it longer.

CHUNKY SPICED APPLE CAKE
(serves 6)

This delicious apple cake is dense, solid, and terribly good. It is loaded with fruit and good spicy flavor and works equally well as a dessert or as a fine breakfast coffeecake. It is one of my favorite things. I eat it right out of the freezer and love it. Use green, tart apples such as Pippins or Granny Smiths for this.

INGREDIENTS:

2 large apples
¾ cup sugar
1 cup flour
1 teaspoon baking powder
½ teaspoon cinnamon
½ teaspoon nutmeg*

1 egg, lightly beaten
½ stick (2 ounces)
    unsalted butter,
    melted and cooled to
    warm
1 teaspoon vanilla

COOKING UTENSIL: An 8 × 8 × 2-inch baking tin, buttered or oiled

PROCEDURE:

1. Preheat oven to 350 degrees.

2. Core apples, but do not peel. Cut into ½-inch cubes. You should have 3 cups. Place in a bowl with sugar, then mix and let sit 5 minutes.

3. Place flour, baking powder, cinnamon, and nutmeg in another bowl. Mix and reserve.

4. Add egg, butter, and vanilla to apples and stir to mix. Add flour mixture and stir until dry ingredients are completely moistened. There will be very little batter and it will be very thick. Scrape out into baking tin, then level somewhat, but let it be rough and irregular, with apples sticking up here and there.

5. Bake in preheated 350-degree oven 45 minutes, or until nicely browned; better overbrowned than under, for the taste.

TO SERVE: Serve warm, room temperature, or chilled. It is good as a dessert served with ice cream.

*Use 1 teaspoon nutmeg if you grate your own.

DO-AHEAD INFORMATION: This keeps 2 or 3 days in the refrigerator or it may be frozen.

APPLE PECAN CAKE
(serves 6 to 8)

This is another chunky apple cake, but in addition to the apples this one also has pecans, raisins, and coconut. It is a great cake and practically a meal in itself.

INGREDIENTS:

12 ounces green, tart apples (2 or 3 apples; 3 cups diced)
½ cup (2 ounces) seedless raisins
1 cup (3 ounces) pecans, ½-inch dice
Rounded ½ cup (2 ounces) coconut
1½ cups all-purpose flour
1 teaspoon baking powder

1 teaspoon cinnamon
½ teaspoon nutmeg*
½ teaspoon powdered ginger
2 eggs
¾ cup granulated sugar
1½ sticks (6 ounces) unsalted butter
1 teaspoon vanilla
Powdered sugar

COOKING UTENSIL: An 8 × 8 × 2-inch baking dish, buttered and floured

PROCEDURE:

1. Preheat oven to 350 degrees.
2. Wash apples, then cut in half and core using a melon

*Double the nutmeg if you are grating your own.

ball scoop. Cut unpeeled apples into ½-inch dice. Mix in a bowl with raisins, pecans, and coconut. Reserve.

3. Place flour, baking powder, cinnamon, nutmeg, and ginger in a bowl and whisk to mix. Reserve.

4. Place eggs and sugar in a bowl and stir to mix. Slice butter, place in a 1-quart glass beaker, and microwave 2 minutes, or cook in saucepan until butter is melted and hot. Beat eggs and sugar at top speed with a hand-held electric mixer for 2 minutes. Add hot butter and beat 20 seconds more. Stir in vanilla, then pour mixture into dry ingredients and stir until blended. Add apple mixture and stir until fruits are coated with the batter, fruitcake style. Dump into baking dish and spread to level.

5. Bake in preheated 350-degree oven for 45 minutes or until nicely browned. Cool in dish on rack. Store in refrigerator.

TO SERVE: Sprinkle with powdered sugar and serve room temperature, as is, or with ice cream or sweetened, flavored whipped cream on the side.

DO-AHEAD INFORMATION: This will keep, refrigerated, 1 or 2 days. Freeze if holding longer.

BLACKBERRY KUCHEN
(serves 8 to 10)

True German *Kuchen* refers to a whole series of pastries made with a sweet, buttery yeast dough. They are generally more like coffeecakes than desserts. This particular nonyeast version is like a tart baked on a cake base. It can be used as a dessert, a marvelous one, or as a coffeecake. The combination of rich butter cake, slightly tart blackberries, and spicy streusel make this a beautiful and delicious pastry.

INGREDIENTS:

THE CAKE:

2 cups all-purpose flour
¾ cup sugar
1 teaspoon baking
   powder

1½ sticks (6 ounces)
   unsalted butter,
   chilled or frozen
3 eggs, chilled

THE FRUIT LAYER:

2 tablespoons flour
4 cups fresh blackberries*

2 tablespoons sugar (or
   more)

THE STREUSEL:

⅓ cup flour
⅓ cup sugar
1 teaspoon cinnamon
½ stick (2 ounces)

unsalted butter,
   chilled or frozen, cut
   in pieces

COOKING UTENSIL: A 12¾ × 9 × 2-inch baking tin or dish

PROCEDURE:

1. Preheat oven to 350 degrees.
2. Place flour, sugar, baking powder, and butter, cut into pieces, into container of food processor fitted with steel

*You could use a 16-ounce package of frozen blackberries instead of fresh; however, when using frozen berries, toss them with ¼ cup flour instead of 2 tablespoons. The frozen berries tend to be very tart, so sprinkle 4 or 5 tablespoons sugar over instead of 2 tablespoons. This kuchen is delicious with raspberries or blueberries. Adjust the sugar according to the sweetness of the fruit.

blade. Process 30 to 60 seconds, or until butter disappears. Add eggs and process 10 seconds, or until dough comes together in a crumbly way. Dump into baking tin and flatten to level, using floured fingers.

3. Place 2 tablespoons flour in a strainer and sprinkle in an even layer over dough. Add blackberries in a single layer, placing them about ½ inch in from the edges unless you have enough to cover the entire surface of the dough. Sprinkle with 2 tablespoons sugar or more.

4. To make the streusel, place 4 ingredients listed in container of food processor fitted with steel blade. Process until mixture forms coarse crumbs. Sprinkle half the streusel over so that the berries still show through. Sprinkle the balance in a thick layer over the edges.

5. Bake in preheated 350-degree oven 45 minutes, or until brown around the edges. Cool on rack.

TO SERVE: Serve room temperature, as is, or with sweetened, flavored whipped cream or vanilla ice cream on the side.

DO-AHEAD INFORMATION: This keeps a day in the room, or 3 or 4 days in the refrigerator.

BROWN SUGAR PECAN SQUARES
(makes 15 2 ½-inch squares or 3 dozen petits fours)

You might call these candylike squares Butterscotch Pecan Brownies. They are rich and delicious with a wonderful brown-sugar taste, very sinful.

INGREDIENTS:

2 cups all-purpose flour

2 teaspoons baking powder

2 cups dark brown sugar, packed down

1 stick (4 ounces) unsalted butter, melted

2 eggs, room temperature

1 teaspoon vanilla

1 cup (4 ounces) pecans, chopped into ¼-inch dice

Powdered sugar

COOKING UTENSIL: A 12¾ × 9 × 2-inch baking tin, buttered

PROCEDURE:

1. Preheat oven to 375 degrees. Measure flour and baking powder, then mix and reserve.

2. Place brown sugar in container of food processor fitted with steel blade. Add melted, hot butter and process 1 minute, scraping sides down once or twice.

3. Add eggs. Process 2 seconds, then scrape down, stir, and process 2 seconds more. Add vanilla and process 2 seconds more.

4. Add flour mixture. Process 2 seconds, then stir and process 2 seconds more. Batter will be very stiff.

5. Add pecans and process 2 seconds. If batter is so thick it stops the machine, knead in pecans by hand.

6. Scrape batter into baking tin and level with wet fingers. The mixture will resemble fudge.

7. Bake in 375-degree oven for 20 minutes, or until nicely browned.

TO SERVE: Sprinkle with powdered sugar and serve as is to accompany a fruit or ice-cream dessert. Cut into 2½-inch squares and serve with a scoop of ice cream on top. Or ice with Cream Cheese Brown Sugar Icing (recipe follows), cut into 1½-inch squares, and serve as petits fours.

DO-AHEAD INFORMATION: These keep 1 or 2 days at room temperature, wrapped air-tight. Freeze if keeping longer.

CREAM CHEESE BROWN SUGAR ICING

This makes just enough for a thin coating over the cake above. If you prefer more icing, double the recipe, doubling all the ingredients except the pecans.

INGREDIENTS:

½ cup dark brown sugar, packed down

1 tablespoon water

4 ounces cream cheese

1 cup (4 ounces) pecans, chopped into ¼-inch dice

PROCEDURE:

1. Place brown sugar and water in a small saucepan. Bring to a boil and let cook 1 minute, stirring.

2. Remove from heat and stir until sugar is dissolved, then allow to cool to warm. (You can speed this up by placing pan in cold water.) Mixture will thicken as it cools.

3. Place cream cheese in mixing bowl, then add warm, thick brown sugar mixture. Stir with spatula, then beat until smooth with whisk or electric mixer.

4. Spread icing over cake and sprinkle with chopped pecans.

LIGHT CARROT ALMOND CAKE
(serves 8 to 10)

Here is a simplified, square cake version of a Viennese-style carrot almond torte that is moist, light, delicate, and completely wonderful. It has no wheat flour at all and contains just a very small amount of cornstarch. Try to use lime, but whether you use lime or lemon when zesting, be careful not to get any of the bitter white part.

INGREDIENTS:

1½ cups (6 ounces) almonds

1 tablespoon cornstarch

Zest of 1 lime or lemon

3 medium carrots (6 ounces), cut in chunks (1½ cups)

3 eggs, warmed by placing in hot water in shells for 5 minutes

¾ cup sugar

1 tablespoon lime or lemon juice

COOKING UTENSIL: A 10¾ × 7 × 1½-inch baking tin, buttered and floured

PROCEDURE:

1. Preheat oven to 350 degrees.

2. Place almonds into container of food processor fitted with steel blade. Process until ground, about 2 minutes. Transfer to a large bowl, then add cornstarch and zest. Mix and reserve.

3. Place carrots in processor and process 1 minute, or until carrots are well grated. Reserve in machine.

4. Put warmed eggs and sugar in a small bowl and beat at highest speed, using a hand-held electric mixer, for 3 minutes, or until mixture is thick and very light in color.

5. Dump carrots into nut mixture, then add lemon juice and beaten eggs all in a heap. Fold quickly but carefully, just until all dry ingredients are moistened. Do not overfold. Pour into prepared tin.

6. Bake in preheated 350-degree oven for 35 minutes or until nicely browned and cake has shrunk away from sides of tin.

TO SERVE: Serve chilled with sweetened whipped cream flavored with lemon or lime. If you have a little more time, make a carrot whipped cream with 1 cup cream, whipped, to which you add ⅔ cup powdered sugar, 3 tablespoons lime or lemon juice, and 1 cup cooked, grated carrot.

DO-AHEAD INFORMATION: This cake seems to be better the second day. It keeps refrigerated for 2 or 3 days and it also freezes well. Be careful handling it; it is delicate.

CHOCOLATE BABA CAKE
(serves 16)

This is one of the best-tasting, most elegant desserts in the whole book. It is a variation of a pastry I learned at the Lenôtre Pastry School outside of Paris. Because I had to fly to France and take classes for a week to capture this beauty, when I teach it I sometimes call it my $1,200 dessert. The dish consists of a chocolate cake square, thoroughly soaked with a rum-flavored syrup, topped with chocolate whipped cream. It's a dessert, not a cake, and it's really good.

INGREDIENTS:

4 eggs
1 cup all-purpose flour
3 tablespoons cocoa, sifted
1 teaspoon baking powder
1 stick (4 ounces) unsalted
    butter
1 cup granulated sugar
    (total)

1 cup water
½ cup rum (dark
    preferred)
8 ounces semisweet
    chocolate*
2 cups whipping cream
¼ cup + 1 tablespoon
    powdered sugar

COOKING UTENSIL: An 8 × 8 × 2-inch baking dish

PROCEDURE:

1. Preheat oven to 375 degrees. Place a strip of foil, shiny side up, across the baking dish so that 2 flaps stick up. This is for easy removal of the cake later.

2. Warm eggs by placing them, in their shells, in a bowl and covering them with hot water. Let sit 5 minutes.

3. Place flour, cocoa, and baking powder in a bowl. Stir with a whisk until mixed. Reserve.

4. Slice butter into pieces and place in a 1-quart glass beaker. Microwave 1½ minutes on high power, or until melted and hot. Place eggs and ½ cup granulated sugar in a small bowl, then beat at top speed with a hand-held electric mixer for 2 minutes. Add the hot butter all at once, then beat another 30 seconds. Pour this mixture into the dry ingredients. Fold, using a wire whisk, until batter is blended and smooth, but do not overfold. Pour into prepared baking dish and tilt to level.

5. Bake in preheated 375-degree oven for 25 minutes. Let cool in dish on rack 1 hour.

*I used Nestlé's real semisweet chocolate morsels.

6. Place remaining ½ cup granulated sugar and 1 cup water in glass beaker. Microwave on high power 3 or 4 minutes or until boiling. Stir to dissolve sugar, then add rum and stir to mix. Pour all at once over cake in dish. When syrup has been absorbed, cover warm cake with plastic and refrigerate 2 hours or until chilled.*

7. Place chocolate in 1-quart glass beaker, then microwave 1½ minutes on full power. Pour in ½ cup cream and microwave another 30 seconds. Whisk until blended and smooth. Add ¼ cup powdered sugar to 1 cup cream, then beat until stiff. Pour still-warm chocolate mixture into whipped cream and whisk until blended. Dump on top of the cake and spread to level. Reserve in refrigerator until serving time.

TO SERVE: Remove cake from dish by lifting up on the foil flaps. Remove foil, then place cake on serving dish and pipe with ½ cup cream that has been whipped stiff with 1 tablespoon powdered sugar. Can be served by cutting cake in half, then slicing halves across into ¾-inch slices. Any leftover cake may be frozen and served another day.

DO-AHEAD INFORMATION: Cake with chocolate cream topping may be kept in refrigerator 2 or 3 days, covered with plastic, or it may be frozen and kept longer. Make sure to defrost before serving, but serve it chilled. Final whipped-cream decoration may be added 2 or 3 hours before serving.

*Normally it is not recommended that hot or warm dishes be covered until they have cooled, but it is suggested in this case so that the rum will not evaporate.

QUEEN OF SHEBA CHOCOLATE SQUARES
(makes 9 2 ¼-inch squares or 3 dozen petits fours)

Here is a simplified, foolproof recipe for one of the richest, most delicious chocolate cake–chocolate glaze squares you ever ate. The special feature of this cake is that it is not completely baked, but is still somewhat raw in the center. This gooey center area sets when it is chilled, however, and becomes the best part. The chocolate glaze that tops these cake squares is so beautiful and easy, you won't believe it.

INGREDIENTS:

3 eggs
⅔ cup all-purpose flour
¼ cup (1 ounce) almonds
1 teaspoon baking
  powder
1 stick + 3 tablespoons
  (5½ ounces) unsalted
  butter

9 ounces real semisweet
  chocolate morsels*
  (total)
½ cup sugar
2 tablespoons rum (dark
  preferred)
1 teaspoon honey (or
  Karo)

COOKING UTENSIL: An 8 × 8 × 2-inch baking tin

PROCEDURE:

1. Preheat oven to 400 degrees. Warm eggs by placing them, in their shells, in a bowl and covering them with hot water. Let sit 5 minutes.

2. Fold an 18-inch-long sheet of aluminum foil so that it measures 7 inches wide. Butter baking tin and place sheet of foil so that it fits tightly across bottom and up the two sides of the dish with two flaps hanging out. Butter the foil. This helps later to remove cake from tin.

*I used Nestlé's, but any semisweet chocolate will do.

3. Place flour, almonds, and baking powder in container of food processor fitted with steel blade. Process 1 minute or until almonds are ground fine. Reserve.

4. Slice 1 stick (4 ounces) butter and place in 1-quart glass beaker with 6 ounces chocolate morsels (1 rounded cup). Microwave 2½ minutes on full power (or melt in saucepan over double boiler), whisking after 2 minutes and again at the end. Transfer to a large bowl and reserve.

5. Place eggs and sugar in a small bowl, then, using a hand-held electric mixer, beat at top speed for 3 minutes. Moving quickly, dump flour-nut mixture all at once on top of chocolate mixture, then dump egg-sugar mixture over all. Add rum, then fold until batter is completely blended, but do not overfold. Dump into prepared baking dish and tilt to level.

6. Bake 17 minutes *exactly* in preheated 400-degree oven. Cake will not be done, but remove it anyway and place, keeping it in the tin, on a rack to cool. As cake cools, press down with your hands to level the top as best you can.

7. When cake has cooled for 1 hour, make glaze. Place 3 ounces chocolate morsels (rounded ½ cup), 3 tablespoons butter, sliced, and honey in a 1-quart glass beaker. Microwave 1 minute on full power, then stir with a spatula until mixture is smooth. Do not overheat and do not whisk as you don't want bubbles. Pour over cake and tilt to cover the top. Don't worry if cake top is not perfectly level. Refrigerate.

TO SERVE: Cut to free cake on flapless sides of tin, then pull flaps carefully and lift out cake. Cut into 9 squares. Serve as is or with ice cream on the side. Or cut into 36 pieces, approximately 1 inch square, and serve as petits fours.

DO-AHEAD INFORMATION: Keeps 2 or 3 days in refrigerator. Caution: because of the underbaking, it is perishable.

CHOCOLATE SAUCE CAKE
(serves 6 to 8)

This is an easy, odd recipe that has been around for years. It's the one in which you pour a cup of boiling water over the batter and when it's baked, there's this cake sitting in chocolate sauce. I've tried working with it to change it one way or another, but with disastrous results. The formula seems to resist tampering. It's a little classic that is meant to be just what it is. If you haven't tried it, give it a whirl. It is ridiculously good.

INGREDIENTS:

1 cup all-purpose flour
½ cup sugar
2 teaspoons baking powder
1½ tablespoons cocoa
Rounded ½ cup

(2 ounces) walnuts, in ¼-inch dice
2 tablespoons unsalted butter
½ cup milk
1 teaspoon vanilla

TOPPING:

¼ cup sugar
½ cup dark brown sugar
3 tablespoons cocoa

1 cup almost boiling water

COOKING UTENSIL: An 8-inch square baking tin

PROCEDURE:

1. Preheat oven to 350 degrees. Place first 5 ingredients in a bowl and mix and reserve.

2. Place butter in a small saucepan and melt. Add milk and heat until just barely warm. Pour into dry ingredients, then add vanilla and stir until thoroughly mixed. Scrape into baking dish and level with spatula.

3. Place first 3 topping ingredients in a bowl. Mix, breaking up any brown-sugar lumps with your fingers, but mixture can be a little lumpy. Distribute over batter in baking tin. Pour 1 cup almost boiling water over all.

4. Bake at 350 degrees 30 to 35 minutes. The shorter baking time gives a runnier chocolate sauce.

TO SERVE: Serve room temperature or warm. Good with ice cream on the side.

DO-AHEAD INFORMATION: Keeps 1 or 2 days in the refrigerator and it freezes very well.

CHOCOLATE SYRUP BUNDT CAKE
WITH GRAND MARNIER
(serves 10 to 12)

This big eight-egg chocolate bundt cake is thoroughly soaked with a rich, Grand Marnier–flavored chocolate syrup. It is a wet, wonderful dessert cake.

INGREDIENTS:

8 eggs

2 cups flour

½ cup cocoa

1 teaspoon baking soda

1 teaspoon baking
    powder

2½ cups sugar (total)

2 sticks (8 ounces)

unsalted butter, room
    temperature, sliced

8 ounces semisweet
    chocolate

1 cup milk

1½ cups orange juice

1 cup + Grand Marnier

½ cup powdered sugar

BAKING UTENSIL: A 3-quart bundt tin (with center tube), approximately 10 inches inside diameter at top and 4 inches high, preferably Teflon coated

PROCEDURE:

1. Preheat oven to 350 degrees. Lightly butter bundt tin and set aside. Place eggs in shells in a large bowl and cover with hot water. Reserve.

2. Measure flour and cocoa loosely into measuring cups and level off. Place flour, cocoa, baking soda, and baking powder in sifter. Sift onto waxed paper, then return to sifter. Reserve.

3. Place 2 cups sugar with butter slices in container of food processor fitted with steel blade. Process 2 minutes, stirring down as necessary. With motor running, add 2 eggs through feed tube. Process 15 seconds, then add 2 more eggs. Continue until all 8 eggs are incorporated. Mixture will be very runny.

4. Sift flour mixture into processor over the batter. Process 2 seconds, then stir and process 2 seconds more. Pour into buttered bundt tin.

5. Bake in preheated 350-degree oven 50 minutes, or until firm to the touch. Don't worry about slightly over-

baking the cake. Remove from oven and cool 15 minutes on a rack.

6. Make soaking syrup by breaking or chopping the semisweet chocolate and place in a saucepan with milk. Bring to a boil, whisking to help melt chocolate. When smooth, add ½ cup sugar and stir to dissolve. Add orange juice and ½ cup Grand Marnier. Stir to mix. Pour or spoon over cake, which will absorb it all.

7. Let cake cool 1 hour, then (optional) spoon ¼ cup Grand Marnier over cake and let it cool another hour. Unmold cake onto a large serving platter, then (optional) spoon another ¼ cup Grand Marnier over the top. Refrigerate uncovered until chilled through. Leave uncovered for several hours or overnight so that the top dries out and the cake can be streaked with icing.

8. To make the icing, loosely measure powdered sugar into measuring cup, then level off and place in a bowl. Add 1 tablespoon Grand Marnier plus 1 teaspoon. Stir with a wire whisk until smooth. The icing needs to be thick enough to have body, but just runny enough to pipe into threads. Add more Grand Marnier if too thick, or more powdered sugar if too thin.

9. Place icing in corner of a freezer-weight, gallon-size plastic food storage bag. Twist bag to gather icing. Poke a hole almost at corner with a round toothpick. Holding bag as if you were milking a cow, make lines radiating from the center of the cake. Refrigerate *uncovered*.

TO SERVE: Serve chilled or at room temperature.

DO-AHEAD INFORMATION: Cake may be baked, soaked, and frozen several weeks ahead. Icing may be added 6 to 8 hours ahead, but make sure cake surface is dry.

NANA'S GINGERBREAD
(serves 8 to 10 or more)

This is a quick version of my grandmother's gingerbread. It is dark, dense, moist, and sweet, and it tastes like Christmas a long time ago. I remember it well from when we were kids and watched her make it in her kitchen. The recipe was rescued by my sister Rosalie Strang, who went to Nana's house a few years before she died and watched her make it.

INGREDIENTS:

2¾ cups flour
1 cup sugar
1 teaspoon baking soda
1 teaspoon cinnamon
½ teaspoon powdered
    ginger
1 teaspoon nutmeg
¼ teaspoon ground cloves

⅛ teaspoon allspice
1 cup (4 ounces) seedless
    raisins
1 cup molasses (dark
    preferred)
1½ cups buttermilk
¾ stick (6 tablespoons)
    unsalted butter*

COOKING UTENSIL: An 8 × 8 × 2-inch baking dish†

PROCEDURE:

1. Preheat oven to 325 degrees.

2. Put flour, sugar, baking soda, and spices into a bowl and stir to mix. Reserve.

3. Place raisins on a sheet of waxed paper. Separate with your fingers and reserve.

*Nana used to use Crisco.
†Nana had a great big, old, black gingerbread pan. It must have been at least 15 × 9 with 3- or 4-inch-high sides. She baked a much larger batch and kept it a long time.

4. Place molasses and buttermilk in a saucepan and heat just to remove the chill. Stir until blended, then reserve.

5. Melt butter in a small saucepan, then pour into baking dish. Swirl it around to butter the dish, then pour into flour mixture. Add molasses mixture also, then whisk well, making sure all flour is completely moistened. Stir in raisins, then dump batter into baking dish.

6. Bake in preheated-350 degree oven for 1 hour, or until done. It should feel firm to the touch. I never quite know when it's done myself, but I know I like it better underdone. Allow to cool in dish on a rack.

TO SERVE: This is really a snack for hungry workingmen or growing kids. However, to serve as a dessert, cut the cake in two (two 4 × 8 cakes), then slice one into ¾-inch pieces, the 4-inch way. Serve on dessert plates with sweetened, flavored whipped cream on the side.

DO-AHEAD INFORMATION: This keeps 3 or 4 days or maybe forever in the room. There are no eggs in it and there is all that sugar and molasses so it's not going to spoil very soon. It seems to me that it tastes better after 1 or 2 days. It freezes very well.

ORANGE LIQUEUR CAKE WITH WALNUTS AND RAISINS
(serves 8)

This is an elegant textured cake with a wonderful flavor. It is very moist because of the orange-liqueur syrup that is poured over it after baking.

INGREDIENTS:

2 eggs

2 cups all-purpose flour

Rounded ½ cup (2 ounces) walnuts, chopped in ¼-inch dice

1 teaspoon baking soda

1 cup seedless raisins

1 stick (4 ounces) unsalted butter

¾ cup buttermilk

1 tablespoon lemon juice

1 teaspoon vanilla

Grated zest of 2 oranges

¾ cup + 2 tablespoons sugar (total)

½ cup orange juice

3–4 tablespoons orange liqueur

COOKING UTENSIL: A 10¾ × 7 × 1½-inch baking tin, buttered and floured

PROCEDURE:

1. Preheat oven to 325 degrees. Warm eggs by placing them, in shells, in a bowl and covering with hot water. Let sit 5 minutes.

2. Place flour, walnuts, and soda in a large bowl. Mix and reserve.

3. Place raisins on a sheet of waxed paper. Separate with your fingers and reserve.

4. Melt butter in a small saucepan. Add buttermilk and heat, if necessary, just until mixture is barely warm. Add lemon juice, vanilla, and zest. Reserve.

5. Place eggs and ¾ cup sugar in a small bowl. Using a hand-held electric mixer, beat at full speed for 3 minutes. Dump buttermilk mixture and beaten egg mixture into flour mixture and fold with a whisk until blended. Mixture must be completely blended, but do not overwork. Stir in raisins. Dump into baking tin and level with a spatula.

6. Bake in preheated 325-degree oven 40 minutes, or

until nicely browned and cake has shrunk slightly from edge of tin.

7. Place 2 tablespoons sugar plus orange juice and orange liqueur in a small saucepan and heat just slightly, stirring, until sugar is dissolved. Pour over the hot cake 5 minutes after it comes out of the oven. Allow to cool in tin on rack.

TO SERVE: Serve at room temperature. If desired, this could be served with sweetened, flavored (orange liqueur) whipped cream.

DO-AHEAD INFORMATION: This cake will keep several days in the refrigerator, and it freezes very well.

PINEAPPLE PECAN UPSIDE-DOWN CAKE
(serves 6 to 8)

This is one of the best things I ever put in my mouth, as they say in the South. I almost might go out on a limb and say that it's my favorite thing in this whole book, but I need to give that one a little more thought. I don't know how this round cake found its way into this otherwise solidly square cake chapter, but this is where it is and it's where it should be. You can bake it in a square tin if you like, but I liked the idea of baking it in the traditional black iron skillet. The bottom of the cake, which becomes the top, has a beautiful arrangement of pineapple slices and pecan halves in a brown sugar–butter glaze. The cake part, wholesome and eggy, is made moist and delicious by the addition of ground pecans and crushed pineapple. You're going to love this.

INGREDIENTS:

1 stick (4 ounces) unsalted
    butter (total)
½ cup (packed) dark
    brown sugar
1 20-ounce can sliced
    pineapple

1 cup (3 ounces) pecans
4 eggs
1 cup flour
1 teaspoon baking powder
¾ cup sugar
1 teaspoon vanilla

COOKING UTENSIL AND SERVING DISH: An old-fashioned cast-iron skillet, 10 inches in diameter at top opening, for baking and a dish or platter with a flat area 10 inches in diameter for serving.

PROCEDURE:

1. Preheat oven to 350 degrees.

2. Melt ½ stick butter in skillet, then, off heat, add brown sugar and stir to mix. Drain pineapple slices, reserving juices for another use. Place 1 ring in center and 6 around sides in an attractive pattern. Chop remaining 3 rings and reserve. Push 18 pecan halves, pretty sides down, into holes of pineapple rings and in spaces between. Reserve balance of pecans.

3. Warm eggs by placing, in shells, in a bowl and covering with hot water. Let sit 5 minutes.

4. Place balance of pecans, flour, and baking powder in container of food processor fitted with steel blade. Process 1 minute or until pecans are ground fine. Transfer to large bowl and reserve.

5. Melt remaining ½ stick butter in a small saucepan and allow to cool to warm.

6. Place eggs and sugar in a small bowl and beat at high speed, using a hand-held electric mixer, for 3 minutes. Add vanilla, chopped pineapple, and warm melted butter and

beat 10 seconds more. Dump into flour-pecan mixture and fold using a wire whisk* or a spatula. Whisk a few strokes now and then to make sure all flour is incorporated and not in lumps, but do not overfold or overwhisk. Dump into skillet on top of pineapple pattern.

7. Bake 30 minutes in 350-degree oven. Cake will be nice and brown and firm to the touch. Remove to a rack and allow to sit 5 minutes, then carefully cut to free the sides of the cake and turn upside down on platter or serving dish. Allow to cool.

TO SERVE: Serve room temperature, as is. There is nothing stopping you from serving sweetened, flavored whipped cream with this, but it isn't necessary.

DO-AHEAD INFORMATION: To be at its best, the cake should be baked, left out in the room, and served within 4 or 5 hours; however, it is still awfully good after being refrigerated a day or two and it freezes well.

FILLED POPPY-SEED CAKE
(12 to 16 servings)

If you like poppy seeds and raisins, you will love this cake, which is elegant and different and delectable. A square poppy-seed cake is split and filled with a poppy-seed–raisin filling, then dusted with powdered sugar, sliced, and served with whipped cream.

*Choose a whisk for this without too many wires, perhaps 12 to 14. The multiwire ones so good for beating egg whites would deflate this batter too much.

INGREDIENTS:

3 eggs
1 stick (4 ounces) unsalted
    butter
2 12½-ounce cans Poppy
    Filling* (total)
1 teaspoon cinnamon
1 teaspoon nutmeg

½ cup milk, room
    temperature
1½ cups all-purpose flour
1 teaspoon baking powder
½ cup sugar
½ cup seedless raisins

COOKING UTENSIL: An 8 × 8 × 2-inch baking dish, buttered

PROCEDURE:

1. Preheat oven to 350 degrees. Warm eggs by placing them, in shells, in a bowl and covering with hot water. Let sit 5 minutes.

2. Melt butter in a small saucepan and allow to cool to warm.

3. Place contents of 1 can of Poppy Filling in a bowl. Add cinnamon and nutmeg and stir to mix. Add milk and stir to blend. Reserve.

4. Mix flour and baking powder in a large bowl. Reserve.

5. Place eggs and sugar in a small bowl. Using a hand-held electric mixer, beat at full speed for 3 minutes. Working quickly, pour melted but still warm butter into eggs and beat 8 to 10 seconds. Right away, pour poppy-seed mixture into flour mixture and dump beaten egg mixture on top. Using a wire whisk,† fold, turning the bowl, then stir and whisk just a little to make sure the flour is not lumpy.

*I used Solo brand.
†Use a whisk with only 12 to 14 wires; too many wires may deflate the batter.

Mixture must be well blended, but do not overwork or it will collapse. Pour batter into baking dish. Tilt to level.

6. Bake in preheated 350-degree oven for 45 minutes or until nicely browned. Allow to cool in dish on a rack.

7. Stir contents of remaining can of Poppy Filling with the raisins. Slice cake into 2 layers, then add filling and replace top layer. Reserve until serving time. If you refrigerate this, do not cover.

TO SERVE: Serve at room temperature or slightly chilled. Cut cake in half to 4 × 8, then sprinkle with powdered sugar and take just half to the table. To serve, slice into ¾-inch-thick slices, with sweetened, flavored whipped cream on the side.

DO-AHEAD INFORMATION: Keeps 2 or 3 days in refrigerator, and it freezes very well.

7

ENTERTAINING TRIFLES

SPICED APPLE BROWNIE TRIFLE

BLUEBERRY TRIFLE

CHOCOLATE TRUFFLE TRIFLE

BAVARIAN CREAM TRIFLE WITH STRAWBERRIES

JELLY ROLL TRIFLE

GRAND MARNIER MERINGUE TRIFLE

PEACH MACAROON TRIFLE

PEAR AND RASPBERRY TRIFLE

PINEAPPLE ANGEL FOOD TRIFLE

This chapter features nine beautiful trifles. They are simple, easy to do, delicious, and elegant enough for the most formal entertaining. The trifle is English in origin and was probably invented to use up a stale spongecake or pound cake. Somebody had the bright idea of breaking up a stale cake, putting it into a glass serving bowl, sprinkling some sherry over it, pouring on some vanilla custard sauce, then adding raspberry jam or fresh fruit. As the top looked a little messy, our hero or heroine decorated it with whipped cream and a few strawberries and *voilà!* the trifle was born. And, it was good!

The quick trifles in this chapter feature all sorts of variations on the one mentioned above. For the cake part, they use ladyfingers, pound cake, chocolate pound cake, or angel food cake. (Whatever cake is used must contain enough eggs so that when it is soaked with cream and liqueur, it does not turn to mush.) For the sauce, most of the trifles use a quick version of the original vanilla custard sauce (English Cream, or *crème anglaise*), but one uses Bavarian cream and a few use melted vanilla or chocolate ice cream to save you even more time. Here's a little advice: in duplicating the melted ice-cream trifles, be sure to choose a good-quality ice cream. Some of the ones I tried (not necessarily the cheapest ones), when melted, had an odd, slightly salty taste that was not pleasant at all.

Trifles in general are not as solid as cakes and will not cut as easily and as neatly. They should be spooned out and served in saucers, somewhat like custards or fruit compotes. Don't be disappointed if they are a bit crumbly. That is their nature.

Note also that when trifles call for rum or orange liqueur, beware of the amounts suggested. Liqueurs and spirits vary in strength, and you and I may not be using the same brand. Try putting in less than the specified amount, then tasting and adding more if desired.

It's time now for the "favorites" game, and in this chapter, I'm really in trouble. There is honestly not one trifle in this group that I don't love. But, as I started this game, I shall continue on with it and will name (in alphabetical order, however) the Blueberry, Bavarian Cream with Strawberries, Pear and Raspberry, and Pineapple Angel Food as my favorites.

SPICED APPLE BROWNIE TRIFLE
(serves 6 to 8)

This trifle doesn't have much class, but it's the easiest one of all to do, and it tastes wonderful.

INGREDIENTS:

1 pint vanilla ice cream,
    melted
3 teaspoons vanilla (total)
3–4 tablespoons rum
1 21-ounce can apple pie
    filling*
1 16-ounce can red sour

pitted cherries,
    water packed
1 13-ounce package
    chocolate brownies†
1 cup whipping cream
2 tablespoons powdered
    sugar

SERVING DISH: An 8-cup glass or crystal serving bowl

PROCEDURE:

1. Place ice cream, 2 teaspoons vanilla, and rum in a large bowl and whisk to mix. Add apple filling (including goo) and drained cherries. Mix well.

2. Cut brownies into ¾-inch squares. Set aside 8 or 9 to use for decoration, then add balance to fruit and stir to mix. Dump into serving bowl and level with spatula. Refrigerate.

3. Whip cream, powdered sugar, and 1 teaspoon vanilla until firm but not too stiff. Ice the trifle with half the cream, then whip the balance stiffer and pipe on top in decorative swirls. Place reserved brownie squares in the swirls. Refrigerate until serving time.

TO SERVE: Serve chilled, as is, spooning it out as you would a fruit compote.

*I used Comstock (Newark, N.Y.).
†I used Sara Lee Chocolate Brownies (frozen). If you can't find them, try a local bakery, or make the ones from the recipe on the Baker's unsweetened chocolate box. They're fast and very good.

DO-AHEAD INFORMATION: Trifle may be prepared 1 or 2 days ahead. Whip cream and finish decorations 4 or 5 hours before serving.

BLUEBERRY TRIFLE
(serves 6 to 8)

Here is a simple blueberry trifle, beautiful, easy, and delicious. I love this.

INGREDIENTS:

2½ cups milk (total)

4 egg yolks

⅓ cup + 2 tablespoons granulated sugar (total)

3 teaspoons vanilla (total)

2 pints fresh blueberries

6 ounces ladyfingers

1 cup whipping cream

2 tablespoons powdered sugar

SERVING DISH: An 8-cup glass or crystal serving bowl

PROCEDURE:

1. Have ready on the side 1 cup cold milk, a clean bowl, and rubber spatula. Place 1½ cups milk, yolks, and ⅓ cup sugar in a saucepan (preferably heavy). Over medium-high heat, whisking occasionally, heat until mixture feels very warm to the touch. Continue cooking, but now whisking all the time, until mixture comes to the *first signs* of a boil (about 4 minutes). You will have to stop whisking now and then to see if there is any bubbling. When you see any bubbles at all, immediately whisk in reserved 1 cup cold milk, then

pour mixture into clean bowl. With rubber spatula, scrape any curdled part from the bottom of the pan, adding it to mixture. Stir in 2 teaspoons vanilla. Reserve.

2. Using a large knife, chop 2 cups blueberries into coarse pieces (could do this in processor), then place in saucepan with 2 tablespoons sugar. Bring to a boil, then add balance of blueberries, stir, and return to the boil. Set aside ⅓ cup of this mixture for decoration later. Reserve balance.

3. Place ⅓ of the ladyfingers in a single layer in bottom of serving bowl. Spoon over ⅓ of the warm cream, then add ½ the blueberries. Add another ⅓ ladyfingers, another ⅓ cream, and another ½ blueberries. Finish with rest of ladyfingers and cream. Press to level the top. Refrigerate until chilled.

4. Whip cream, powdered sugar, and 1 teaspoon vanilla until firm but not too stiff. Ice the trifle with half the cream, then whip balance stiffer and pipe 6 large decorative swirls around the outside edge and 1 in the center, making slight depressions in the center of each. Spoon 5 or 6 reserved berries into each depression. Reserve in refrigerator until serving time.

TO SERVE: Serve chilled, as is.

DO-AHEAD INFORMATION: Trifle may be prepared 1 or 2 days ahead. Keep refrigerated. Whip cream and do final decorations 4 or 5 hours before serving. *Note:* Because of the egg yolks, this trifle is perishable; do not keep refrigerated more than 3 days.

CHOCOLATE TRUFFLE TRIFLE
(serves 6 to 8)

This dessert, which is basically just an assembly job, has amazingly good quality. Part of the secret is the bolstering of commercial chocolate ice cream with an extra ounce of unsweetened chocolate. The rest is that the recipe is simple and the ingredients that go into it are good. You can make this recipe even easier by using commercial chocolate truffles, if you can find (and afford) them.

INGREDIENTS:

2 ounces semisweet chocolate

1 cup whipping cream (total)

¼ cup + 1½ teaspoons rum (total)

4 tablespoons powdered sugar (total)

1 quart chocolate ice cream, melted

1 ounce unsweetened chocolate, chopped

1 10¾-ounce chocolate pound cake,* cut in ¼-inch slices

1 29-ounce + 1 16-ounce can pear halves in syrup, drained, cut in ¼-inch slices

1 teaspoon vanilla

SERVING DISH: An 8-cup glass or crystal serving bowl

PROCEDURE:

1. To make the chocolate truffles, place 2 ounces semi-sweet chocolate (scant ½ cup morsels) in a glass beaker. Add 1 tablespoon cream, 1½ teaspoons rum, and 2 table-

*I used Sara Lee Chocolate Pound Cake. If you can't find that, use Sara Lee All-Butter Pound Cake or any good pound cake.

spoons powdered sugar. Microwave 1 minute on high, then whisk until smooth. Spread on a plate and refrigerate 30 minutes, or until firm.

2. Place ¼ cup melted chocolate ice cream plus un-sweetened chocolate in glass beaker. Microwave 30 seconds, then whisk until smooth, heating again in microwave if necessary. Pour into melted chocolate ice cream along with ¼ cup rum. Mix well. Pour enough in bottom of serving dish to moisten. Add ⅓ of the pound cake slices in a single layer, then more chocolate cream, ½ of the pear slices, more chocolate cream, another ⅓ cake slices, chocolate, pears, cake slices, and the rest of the chocolate cream. Press down to consolidate. Refrigerate.

3. Divide the chocolate truffle mixture into 8 portions. Pinch portions to stick together, then roll into balls. Reserve in refrigerator.

4. Whip balance of cream with 2 tablespoons powdered sugar plus 1 teaspoon vanilla to medium stiff (you could also flavor this with some crème de cacao). Spread half on top of the trifle, then whip balance stiffer and pipe 6 or 8 rosettes on top. Place chocolate truffles in the rosettes. Refrigerate until serving time.

TO SERVE: Sift a tiny bit of powdered sugar over the truffles. If desired, scrape chocolate curls in center (see Grapes in Rum Butterscotch Cream). Serve chilled, spooning out portions as neatly as possible.

DO-AHEAD INFORMATION: The truffles may be made weeks ahead. The trifle may be assembled 1 or 2 days ahead. Do the final whipped-cream decorations 5 to 6 hours before serving.

BAVARIAN CREAM TRIFLE WITH STRAWBERRIES
(serves 8)

This is a heavenly dessert, consisting of an orange liqueur Bavarian cream, strawberries, and soaked ladyfingers. It is a simplified variation of a dish I learned in the summer of 1968, working in a pastry shop in Blois, in the château country of France. The *pâtissier,* Yves La Porte, and his wife, Brigitte, now own a hotel in Metz called Le Globe. Yves is a wonderful pastry chef and they are both charming and lovely people.

INGREDIENTS:

2 pints strawberries
3 tablespoons cold water
1½ envelopes gelatin
2 cups milk (total)
¾ cup granulated sugar
6 egg yolks
3 teaspoons vanilla (total)

5 tablespoons orange liqueur (or more or less, to taste)
2 cups whipping cream (total)
3 ounces ladyfingers
2 tablespoons powdered sugar

SERVING DISH: An 8-cup glass or crystal serving bowl

PROCEDURE:

1. Select 13 or 14 medium, uniform, attractive strawberries and set aside for decoration. Brush (or wash and dry well) the balance, to be used in the dessert, and reserve in refrigerator.

2. Place water and gelatin (3 rounded teaspoons) in a cup. Stir and reserve.

3. Have ready on the side ½ cup cold milk, a clean bowl (preferably metal), and a rubber spatula. Put 1½ cups milk,

yolks, and granulated sugar in a saucepan (preferably heavy). Place over medium-high heat and, whisking occasionally, heat until mixture feels very warm to the touch. Continue cooking, but now whisking all the time, until the mixture shows the *first signs* of boiling (4 or 5 minutes). You will have to stop whisking now and then to look. When you see the first bubbles, immediately whisk in reserved ½ cup cold milk, then pour mixture into a clean bowl. Using rubber spatula, scrape any curdled part from the bottom of the pan, adding it to the mixture. Right away, add gelatin and whisk to dissolve. Stir in 2 teaspoons vanilla, orange liqueur, and 1 cup cream. Reserve.

4. Place the bowl of hot cream into a larger bowl containing 1 or 2 inches of ice water (more ice than water). Allow cream to cool from hot to warm, stirring occasionally. Meanwhile, hull the strawberries to be used in the dessert.

5. When the cream feels just warm to the touch, pour ⅓ of it into the serving bowl. Squeeze each strawberry to crush it a little while adding ⅓ of them to the cream. Place ½ the ladyfingers on top, split, in a single layer. Push them down to embed them in the cream. Add more cream, another ⅓ squeezed strawberries, the rest of the ladyfingers, the rest of the cream, and the rest of the squeezed strawberries. Level as best you can. Reserve in refrigerator 5 or 6 hours or overnight.

6. To decorate, whip the remaining 1 cup cream with 1 teaspoon vanilla and powdered sugar until stiff. Spread half the cream over the trifle, mounding it slightly in the center. Top with some halved, reserved strawberries in a pretty pattern, then place one whole strawberry in the center. You may stop there, or pipe the rest of the whipped cream in rosettes here and there. Reserve in refrigerator.

TO SERVE: Serve chilled, as is.

DO-AHEAD INFORMATION: The dessert may be prepared a day ahead. Whip the cream and decorate 5 or 6 hours before serving.

JELLY ROLL TRIFLE
(serves 6 to 8)

This really isn't a jelly roll trifle. It started out being one, but I couldn't find a decent commercial jelly roll, so I had to improvise a pound-cake one. It works great. I also finally found some fairly good strawberries (by June 24) and, putting this trifle all together, my, is it good! It's also very pretty with the "jelly roll" slices lining the outside of the glass bowl. If you can find a good bakery jelly roll, buy it and you'll save yourself a little extra work.

INGREDIENTS:

2½ cups milk (total)
4 egg yolks
⅓ cup granulated sugar
3 teaspoons vanilla (total)
1 10¾-ounce pound cake*
10 ounces red raspberry
    jelly†

2 pints ripe strawberries
3 ounces ladyfingers
1 cup whipping cream
2 tablespoons powdered
    sugar

*I used Sara Lee All-Butter Pound Cake.
†Red currant jelly could be used instead. It is better to use one of the acidic red jellies, such as raspberry or currant, as they cut the sweetness of the dish.

SERVING DISH: An 8-cup glass or crystal serving bowl

PROCEDURE:

1. Have ready on the side 1 cup cold milk, a clean bowl, and a rubber spatula. Place 1½ cups milk, yolks, and granulated sugar in a saucepan (preferably heavy). Over medium-high heat, whisking occasionally, heat until mixture feels very warm to the touch. Continue cooking, but now whisking all the time, until mixture shows the *first signs* of boiling (4 or 5 minutes). You will have to stop whisking now and then to look. When you see the first bubbles, immediately whisk in reserved 1 cup cold milk, then pour mixture into clean bowl. With rubber spatula, scrape any curdled part from the bottom of the pan and add to mixture. Stir in 2 teaspoons vanilla. Reserve.

2. Line bottom and sides of bowl with ¼-inch-thick slices of jelly roll, or do the following: Slice pound cake into ¼-inch slices (about 25 slices), keeping slices in sequence. Divide into 3 equal stacks. Place raspberry jelly in a bowl and whisk until runny and smooth. Spoon 1½ teaspoons jelly on 1 pound-cake slice and spread just short of edges. Put another slice on top and press down firmly to join. Continue until the 3 cake stacks are finished. Slice down the stacks in ¼-inch slices. Line bottom and sides of bowl with the slices up to the 8-cup level.

3. Set aside 8 attractive strawberries plus 1 larger (center) one to be used for decoration. Brush (or wash and dry) and hull the balance and cut into ⅛-inch slices. Place a layer of strawberry slices (about ⅓) into cake-lined bowl. Add some vanilla cream, a single layer of ladyfinger halves, more cream, more sliced berries, the rest of the ladyfingers, the rest of the cream, the rest of the berries, and, finally, cover the top with the bits and pieces of leftover pound-cake slices. Press down to level. Reserve in refrigerator.

4. Whip cream, powdered sugar, and 1 teaspoon vanilla until firm but not too stiff. Ice the trifle with ½ the cream, then whip balance stiffer and pipe 8 decorative rosettes around the outside edge and 1 in the center. Brush (or wash and dry well) and hull the reserved strawberries and place in the rosettes. Reserve in refrigerator until serving time.

TO SERVE: Serve chilled, as is.

DO-AHEAD INFORMATION: Trifle may be prepared 1 or 2 days ahead. Keep refrigerated. Whip cream and do final decoration 4 or 5 hours before serving. *Note:* This trifle is perishable because of the egg yolks. Do not keep refrigerated more than 3 days.

GRAND MARNIER MERINGUE TRIFLE
(serves 6 to 8)

This delicious trifle is a variation of *charlotte portugaise,* a dessert I learned at the Cordon Bleu in Paris a few years back. It was, and probably still is, one of their most wonderful creations. The taste of this quick, ladyfinger version is amazingly close to the Cordon Bleu original. It is a beautiful and fabulous dessert.

INGREDIENTS:
2½ cups milk (total)
4 egg yolks
⅓ cup + 5 tablespoons

granulated sugar
(total)
2 teaspoons vanilla

5 to 6 tablespoons Grand
    Marnier*
Zest of 1 or 2 oranges
    (optional)
6 ounces ladyfingers

2 egg whites (may be
    chilled)
2 ounces sliced almonds
Powdered sugar

SERVING DISH: A 9-inch ovenproof glass pie dish

PROCEDURE:

1. Preheat oven to 425 degrees.

2. Have ready on the side 1 cup cold milk, a clean bowl, and a rubber spatula. Place 1½ cups milk, egg yolks, and ⅓ cup granulated sugar in a saucepan (preferably heavy). Over medium-high heat, whisking occasionally, heat until mixture feels very warm to the touch. Continue cooking, but now whisking all the time, until mixture shows the *first signs* of a boil (4 or 5 minutes). You will have to stop whisking now and then to look. When you see the first bubbles, immediately whisk in reserved 1 cup cold milk, then pour mixture into clean bowl. With rubber spatula, scrape any curdled part from the bottom of the pan, adding it to mixture. Whisk in vanilla, orange liqueur, and (optional) zest.

3. Place ⅓ of the ladyfingers in a single layer in bottom of pie dish. Spoon over ⅓ of warm cream, then add another ⅓ ladyfingers, another ⅓ cream, and finish with final layer of ladyfingers and rest of the cream. Wipe off pie dish rim so that it is clean and dry.

4. Place egg whites and 3 tablespoons granulated sugar in a small bowl and, using a hand-held electric mixer, beat at high speed for 2 or 3 minutes or until stiff (mixture stays in bowl when held upside down). Add 2 tablespoons sugar

*Cointreau also works fine for this; and a domestic Triple Sec would be acceptable, but not very exciting.

and beat 4 to 5 seconds more. Dump onto trifle and spread with a knife to a smooth coat. Sprinkle sliced almonds over all, then sift a light coating of powdered sugar on top.

5. Bake in preheated 425-degree oven 8 or 9 minutes, or until almonds are toasted and meringue has browned. Allow to cool, then reserve in refrigerator until serving time.

TO SERVE: Serve chilled, as is.

DO-AHEAD INFORMATION: This may be prepared 1 or 2 days ahead, or it may be frozen and kept longer. This dessert is very perishable. Do not keep refrigerated for more than 3 days and, even frozen, do not keep longer than 2 weeks.

PEACH MACAROON TRIFLE
(serves 6 to 8)

Fresh, ripe peaches and good-quality coconut macaroons make this trifle a little different, and very good. If good peach ice cream is available, use it instead of vanilla.

INGREDIENTS:

1 quart vanilla ice cream, melted

3 teaspoons vanilla (total)

4–5 tablespoons orange liqueur

4½ ounces coconut macaroons*

5 medium peaches (1⅔ pounds)

2 teaspoons granulated sugar

*I used 3 Pepperidge Farm Coconut Macaroon Snack Bars. They come in 9¼-ounce packages of 6 bars. Eat the other 3. If you can't find these, use any soft coconut or almond macaroon.

3–4 ounces ladyfingers
1 cup whipping cream

2 tablespoons powdered
   sugar

SERVING DISH: An 8-cup glass or crystal serving bowl

PROCEDURE:

   1. Place ice cream, 2 teaspoons vanilla, and orange liqueur in a bowl and whisk to mix.

   2. Cut macaroons into ¼-inch dice and reserve.

   3. Wash, then slice 2 peaches (I don't peel) into thin slices. Place in a bowl, sprinkle with granulated sugar, and reserve in refrigerator for decoration later. Wash and slice remaining peaches and cut into smaller, bite-size pieces. Reserve.

   4. Pour a little vanilla cream into bottom of serving bowl. Place ⅓ of the ladyfingers in a single layer in bottom of bowl. Add a little more cream, then ½ the macaroon pieces and ½ the bite-size peach pieces. Add more cream, another ⅓ ladyfingers, more cream, the rest of the macaroon and peach pieces, more cream, rest of ladyfingers and rest of cream. Press down with a spatula to level. Refrigerate.

   5. Whip cream, powdered sugar, and 1 teaspoon vanilla until firm, but not too stiff (could flavor with orange liqueur). Ice the trifle with half the cream, then whip balance stiff and pipe on top in decorative swirls. Just before serving, arrange reserved peach slices on top.

TO SERVE: Serve chilled, as is, spooning trifle out as you would a fruit compote.

DO-AHEAD INFORMATION: Trifle may be prepared 1 day ahead. Slice peaches for decoration and whip the cream 4 or 5 hours before serving.

PEAR AND RASPBERRY TRIFLE
(serves 6 to 8)

The combination of very cold pears, raspberries, English Cream, and orange liqueur–soaked ladyfingers makes this dessert refreshing and ambrosial. It is also very lovely and it's fun to make because, for an elaborate dessert like this, it goes fast and is mostly an assembly job. The trifle is a little expensive, but it is worth it because of its spectacular appearance and wonderful taste.

INGREDIENTS:

1½ cups milk

4 egg yolks

¼ cup granulated sugar

2 teaspoons vanilla (total)

4 tablespoons Cointreau* (total, optional)

2 10-ounce packages frozen raspberries, in heavy syrup, defrosted

6 ounces ladyfingers

1 29-ounce can pears in syrup, drained, cut ¼-inch thick

1 cup whipping cream

2 teaspoons powdered sugar

SERVING DISH: An 8-cup glass or crystal serving bowl

PROCEDURE:

1. Have ready on the side ½ cup cold milk, a clean bowl, and a rubber spatula. Place 1 cup milk, yolks, and granulated sugar in a saucepan (preferably heavy). Over medium-high heat, whisking occasionally, heat until mixture feels very warm to the touch. Continue cooking, but now whisking all the time, until mixture shows the *first signs* of boiling (3 to 4 minutes). You will have to stop whisking

*You may substitute Grand Marnier, or a domestic Triple Sec.

now and then to look. When you see the first bubbles, immediately whisk in reserved ½ cup cold milk, then pour mixture into clean bowl. Using rubber spatula, scrape any curdled part from the bottom of the pan, adding it to mixture. Stir in 1 teaspoon vanilla. Whisk, then let cool and add 2 tablespoons (optional) Cointreau. Reserve.

2. Drain and reserve raspberries carefully, keeping them whole. Reserve ½ cup raspberry juice, then add 2 tablespoons Cointreau, if using. This is the soaking syrup. Select 8 or 9 whole raspberries and reserve them, separated, in freezer for decoration.

3. Pull apart ladyfingers and dip flat surface of ⅓ of them very quickly into the soaking syrup and place in bottom of serving bowl, soaked side up, in a solid layer. Pour ½ cup reserved custard cream over them, then add all the drained, sliced pears in an even layer. Arrange another ⅓ of dipped ladyfingers over the pears, dipped side down this time, then add 1 cup of the custard cream and all the raspberries in an even layer. Be sure to place some raspberries at the edge of the bowl so that they show through the glass. Add a final layer of dipped ladyfingers and rest of custard cream. Spread evenly, then press down to compact a bit. Refrigerate.

4. Whip cream, powdered sugar, and 1 teaspoon vanilla until thick but not too stiff. Ice the trifle with ½ the cream, then whip balance stiffer and pipe a design on top. Reserve in refrigerator.

TO SERVE: Place frozen reserved raspberries on trifle. Serve chilled.

DO-AHEAD INFORMATION: Trifle may be prepared 1 or 2 days ahead. Keep refrigerated. Whip cream and decorate

4 or 5 hours before serving. This dessert is perishable; keep it refrigerated and do not keep more than 3 days.

PINEAPPLE ANGEL FOOD TRIFLE
(serves 8)

This easy and delightful trifle is made of sherry-soaked angel food cake slices, pineapple, bananas, and melted vanilla ice cream. It is decorated with whipped cream, pineapple rings, and glacéed cherries that have been soaked in rum. You will be happy to hear that it is strictly an assembly job; there is no cooking at all. The dessert works very well for casual entertaining, but is also glamorous enough to be presented at the most formal dinner.

INGREDIENTS:

1 quart vanilla ice cream*
3 teaspoons vanilla (total)
10 ounces angel food cake†
½ cup sherry**
¼ cup water

3 tablespoons powdered sugar (total)
1 20-ounce can sliced pineapple
2 large bananas
1 cup whipping cream
Glacéed cherries

*Try to get French-style vanilla ice cream (containing eggs), if possible.
†To do this right, you should make your own or buy a good one from a quality bakery. If necessary, you can get by with one of those loaf-shaped angel food cakes from the supermarket, but read the label and if the additives list is too horrible, use a good pound cake instead.
**I used a California cream sherry, but any good sherry will do. Taste and add more powdered sugar if the sherry is not very sweet.

SERVING DISH: An attractive glass serving bowl with an 8-cup capacity

PROCEDURE:

1. Melt ice cream. Stir in 2 teaspoons vanilla and reserve.

2. Cut cake into slices ½-inch thick, or break tube cake into walnut-size chunks with an angel-cake cutter or 2 forks. Spread out on a dish or platter. Make soaking syrup by placing sherry, water, and 1 tablespoon powdered sugar into a cup and stirring to dissolve sugar. Pour over cake pieces, turning them until they have soaked up all the liquid. Reserve.

3. Reserve 4 pineapple rings for decoration. Cut balance into small, bite-size pieces. Slice bananas. Reserve.

4. Assemble in 2 or 3 layers, depending on shape of serving dish. Place a layer of cake in bottom of dish. Pour some melted ice cream over, then add pineapple pieces and banana slices. Continue until ingredients are used and dish is filled. Refrigerate.

5. To decorate, whip cream with 2 tablespoons powdered sugar plus 1 teaspoon vanilla. Frost top of trifle with part of cream, then decorate with half or whole pineapple rings, glacéed cherries (optional: soak cherries in rum 1 or 2 hours or more), and the rest of the cream piped on top.

TO SERVE: Serve chilled as is.

DO-AHEAD INFORMATION: Trifle may be prepared 1 or 2 days ahead and kept in refrigerator. Or it may be frozen for a week. Whip cream and decorate 4 or 5 hours before serving.

8

SPECTACULAR CAKE DESSERTS

ALMOND MOCHA TORTE

BLUEBERRY MOUNTAIN CAKE

CHERRY DOME CAKE

CHOCOLATE CREAM CAKE

CHOCOLATE MOUSSE CAKE WITH STRAWBERRIES

CHOCOLATE MOUSSE LOAF

SPICED PECAN TORTE WITH BANANAS

WALNUT TORTE WITH PEACHES AND CREAM

In this chapter and in the next one on Spectacular *Light* Cake Desserts you will find the biggest, most beautiful, most spectacular desserts in the book. They are not necessarily any more fabulous than the other desserts, but they are grander and more impressive. If you have an important meal that you want to finish with a real bang, these dessert cakes will do it.

These spectacular cake desserts are outstanding not only from a visual standpoint but also from the standpoint of taste. You will find that they taste not only as good as they look but perhaps even better.

Here are my favorites in this chapter in order of preference: Chocolate Cream Cake, Cherry Dome Cake, Walnut Torte with Peaches and Cream, Spiced Pecan Torte with Bananas, and Almond Mocha Torte.

ALMOND MOCHA TORTE
(serves 8 to 10)

This is a wonderful coffee-chocolate-almond torte. It consists of light, ground almond cake layers, moistened with coffee syrup, filled with fine chocolate bits in coffee whipped cream. The torte is iced and decorated with coffee whipped cream and topped with easy chocolate curls.

INGREDIENTS:

THE CAKE:

4 eggs
⅔ cup (3 ounces) almonds
1 cup flour
1 teaspoon baking
   powder

½ stick (2 ounces)
   unsalted butter,
   chilled or frozen
¾ cup sugar
1 teaspoon vanilla

SOAKING SYRUP:

1½ cups water
2 tablespoons instant
   coffee*

3 tablespoons sugar

FILLING AND TOPPING:

2 cups whipping cream
6 ounces semisweet
   chocolate†
6 teaspoons instant coffee
   (total)

6 tablespoons powdered
   sugar (total)
3 tablespoons water

COOKING UTENSIL: For a change, I like to do this in a square form, baking the cake in an 8 × 8 × 2-inch baking

*I used Medaglia d'Oro instant espresso coffee.
†I used 1 rounded cup of Nestlé's real semisweet chocolate morsels.

dish. If you prefer, bake the cake in an 8-inch springform pan. In either case, butter and flour the utensil.

PROCEDURE:

1. Preheat oven to 350 degrees. Warm eggs by placing them, in shells, in a bowl and covering with hot water. Let sit 5 minutes.

2. Place almonds, flour, and baking powder in container of food processor fitted with steel blade. Process 1 minute or until nuts are ground fine. Transfer to a large bowl and reserve.

3. Melt butter in a small saucepan and allow to cool to warm.

4. Place eggs and ¾ cup sugar in a small bowl and, using a hand-held electric mixer, beat at high speed for 3 minutes, or until mixture is pale and thick. Add warm melted butter and vanilla and beat 10 seconds more. Pour all at once into flour mixture and fold, using a wire whisk. Whisk for a few beats at the end to make sure the flour is completely incorporated, but do not overwork. Pour into baking dish or tin.

5. Bake in preheated 350-degree oven for 30 minutes, or until nicely browned and cake feels firm to the touch. Place dish or tin on rack and allow to cool 5 minutes. Turn cake out onto rack and allow to finish cooling.

6. Place syrup ingredients in a small saucepan. Heat, stirring, until coffee is dissolved and mixture comes just to the boil. Allow to cool.

7. Whip cream until stiff but still slightly runny. Divide cream into 2 equal batches. Set 1 batch aside, then, into the second, place chocolate, chopped fairly fine (could do this in food processor), 2 teaspoons instant coffee, and 2 tablespoons powdered sugar. Whisk to mix.

8. Slice cake into 2 layers. Place bottom layer on a

serving dish. Spoon ½ of the coffee soaking syrup over the bottom cake layer, then add all the cream just prepared and spread evenly. Place second cake layer on top, then spoon over remaining soaking syrup.

9. Place 3 tablespoons water plus 4 teaspoons instant coffee in small saucepan and bring just to the boil, stirring to dissolve the coffee. Let cool for 2 or 3 minutes, then add to remaining whipped cream along with 4 tablespoons powdered sugar. Set aside some of this cream for piping, then ice top and sides of the cake with the balance. Cover cake with plastic, then refrigerate it along with remaining cream.

10. Using a pastry bag, pipe decorations with remaining coffee whipped cream. Scrape and add chocolate curls here and there (see Grapes in Rum Butterscotch Cream).

TO SERVE: Serve chilled with cups of good coffee. To serve square cake, cut in half, then slice halves across into pieces 1 to 1½ inches thick.

DO-AHEAD INFORMATION: Cake layers could be done weeks ahead and frozen. Cake could be assembled, except for final piped decorations, then wrapped well in plastic and kept in refrigerator 1 or 2 days or frozen. Add decorations 3 to 5 hours before serving.

BLUEBERRY MOUNTAIN CAKE
(serves 8 to 12)

This cake features a great mountain of blueberries with a snowy peak of whipped cream on top. It is actually a kind of blueberry shortcake, or short torte, if you prefer. It is moist, delicious, and wonderful.

INGREDIENTS:

THE CAKE:

½ stick (2 ounces) unsalted butter

2 ounces pecans

1 cup all-purpose flour

1 teaspoon baking powder

4 eggs, room temperature

¾ cup sugar

1 teaspoon vanilla

1 cup frozen blueberries (defrosted)

FILLING AND TOPPING:

2 16-ounce packages frozen blueberries (or 2 pints fresh)*

⅓ cup granulated sugar

2 teaspoons lemon juice

1 cup whipping cream

2 tablespoons powdered sugar

1 teaspoon vanilla

COOKING UTENSILS: 2 8-inch round cake tins, well buttered, lightly floured

PROCEDURE:

1. Preheat oven to 350 degrees. Melt butter and reserve.

2. Place pecans, flour, and baking powder into container of food processor fitted with steel blade. Process 1 minute, or until nuts are ground fairly fine. Reserve.

3. Place eggs, sugar, and vanilla in a bowl and stir to mix. Using a hand-held electric mixer, beat at top speed 2 or 3 minutes, or until mixture is thick, light, and fluffy. Add warm butter and beat 10 seconds more. Add nut mixture and incorporate into the eggs, using mixer at lowest speed. Stir in blueberries (swipe these from the frozen or fresh blueberries to be used in the filling). Divide batter equally in cake tins, and tilt and jiggle to level.

4. Bake in preheated 350-degree oven 30 minutes, or

*Or you could use 3 16-ounce cans of blueberries. Drain, then return ¾ cup syrup to the berries, discarding rest of juice. Add 2 teaspoons lemon juice, if desired.

until nicely browned. Let cool in tins on racks 15 minutes, then turn cakes out and finish cooling on racks.

FILLING AND FINISHING THE CAKE:

1. Place 1½ cups frozen or fresh berries plus granulated sugar and lemon juice into container of food processor fitted with steel blade. Process 1 minute or until blueberries are puréed.

2. Place mixture in a saucepan along with balance of berries. Bring to a boil, stirring occasionally, then let cook 2 or 3 minutes. Transfer to a large bowl and allow to cool (you can hurry this up by placing bowl in freezer, uncovered, for 1 hour).

3. To assemble, place 1 cake layer on a serving dish. Prick all over with a toothpick to allow juices to soak in. Spoon ½ the blueberries with juice into center of cake, allowing a minute for some of the juices to soak in. Level berries, then add second cake layer. Prick, then add balance of blueberry mixture in center of cake. Wait 1 minute, then arrange berries to look like a big mountain.

4. Whip cream, not too stiff, with powdered sugar and vanilla. Reserve in refrigerator.

TO SERVE: Serve chilled, right out of the refrigerator. Just before serving, stir or whip cream to get it back together, then dump out and shape a large blob on top so that the whole thing looks like a snowcapped mountain.

DO-AHEAD INFORMATION: The cake layers may be done ahead and frozen. The cream may be whipped 8 hours ahead or longer. The cake itself is at its best assembled 3 or 4 hours before eating. It loses its wetness and its excitement if assembled much farther ahead than that.

CHERRY DOME CAKE
(serves 8 to 12)

Here comes another goodie. The Apple Pecan Cake from Chapter 6 (apples, pecans, raisins, coconut) is here reduced, rounded, and dressed up so elegantly that it can be presented at the fanciest occasion. The wonderful, chunky cake is topped with a dome of pie cherries in whipped cream, then surrounded by a lovely whipped-cream, cherry décor. This is one of the prettiest and best-tasting cakes in the book.

INGREDIENTS:

1 large, green, tart apple (2 cups diced)

⅓ cup raisins

2 ounces pecans (⅔ cup), ½-inch dice

⅓ cup coconut, shredded or flaked

1 cup all-purpose flour

1 teaspoon baking powder

1 teaspoon cinnamon

¼ teaspoon nutmeg

½ teaspoon powdered ginger

1 stick (4 ounces) unsalted butter*

2 eggs, room temperature

½ cup granulated sugar

1 teaspoon vanilla

1 cup whipping cream (total)

2 tablespoons powdered sugar

20 ounces cherry pie filling†

*You may use ½ cup vegetable oil instead of butter. I tried it and it works fine. The texture of the cake is even softer and nicer, but the cake tastes much better to me made with butter.
†I used Comstock, and I know what you're thinking, but the only other cherries available here are the water-pack sour cherries, which I find so tart that they're unpleasant. I would prefer sour pie cherries packed in syrup, but I can't find them.

COOKING UTENSIL: An 8-inch round cake tin with 1¾-inch sides, well buttered and lightly floured

PROCEDURE:

1. Preheat oven to 350 degrees. Core and cut unpeeled apple into ½-inch dice. Mix in a bowl with raisins, pecans, and coconut. Reserve.

2. Place flour, baking powder, cinnamon, nutmeg, and ginger in a bowl and whisk to mix. Reserve.

3. Melt butter and reserve. Place eggs, granulated sugar, and vanilla in a bowl and stir to mix. Using a hand-held electric mixer, beat at top speed 2 minutes, or until mixture is light and fluffy. Add warm butter and beat 20 seconds more. Pour batter into flour mixture and stir until blended. Add apple mixture and stir until fruits are coated with the batter. Dump into cake tin and spread to level.

4. Bake in preheated 350-degree oven 35 to 40 minutes, or until nicely browned but not too dark. Do not overbake or cake can be dry. Let cool in tin on a rack for 15 minutes, then unmold and allow to finish cooling.

5. To assemble cake, beat cream with powdered sugar until stiff, but not overbeaten. Place cake layer on serving plate, then ice with a thin layer of the whipped cream. Reserve balance of cream.

6. Place cherry pie filling in coarse sieve and bang against rim of a large bowl. Discard red paste. Reserve 13 prettiest cherries for decoration. Place balance of cherries in a bowl. Stir in ½ cup sweetened whipped cream. Place in center of cake. Cover with plastic and help shape into an even mound. (Try inverting a small rice bowl or saucer and pressing down on the mound.) Peel off plastic. Smooth icing again, then pipe 12 rosettes of whipped cream around

mound and 1 on top. Place a reserved cherry in each rosette. Reserve in refrigerator.

TO SERVE: Remove from refrigerator 1 hour before serving.

DO-AHEAD INFORMATION: Cake layer may be made ahead and kept well-wrapped in a cool place for 2 or 3 days. I have frozen it, but it has sometimes been crumbly on slicing later, so I'm not sure that it's advisable. Assemble and decorate 6 to 8 hours before serving.

CHOCOLATE CREAM CAKE
(serves 10 to 12)

Here is another favorite of mine, four chocolate cake layers with a moist chocolate cream filling, topped with whipped cream and pulled chocolate lines. It is a light, divine cake, and an easy one in that the cake layers are done completely in the food processor.

INGREDIENTS:

1⅓ cups cake flour
1 teaspoon baking *soda*
3 ounces unsweetened chocolate
1⅓ cups granulated sugar
½ stick (2 ounces) unsalted butter
3 eggs, slightly warmed

⅔ cup milk, slightly warmed
1 teaspoon vanilla
9 ounces semisweet chocolate (total)
3 cups whipping cream (total)
½ cup + 2 tablespoons powdered sugar (total)

COOKING UTENSILS: 2 8-inch baking tins, well buttered, lightly floured

PROCEDURE FOR CAKE LAYERS:

1. Preheat oven to 350 degrees. Mix flour and soda in a sifter. Reserve.

2. Cut unsweetened chocolate into chunks and place with granulated sugar in food processor fitted with steel blade. Process 1 or 2 minutes, or until chocolate is ground almost powdery fine. Melt butter, then add to chocolate in processor and process 2 minutes, stirring once or twice. Add eggs, then pulse 5 or 6 times. Stir, then pulse 5 or 6 times more. Add milk and vanilla. Stir, then process 2 seconds, then stir again and process 2 seconds more. Add flour mixture and process 2 seconds, then stir. Pour into prepared cake tins. Tilt and jiggle to level the batter.

3. Bake in preheated 350-degree oven 25 to 30 minutes, or until cakes feel firm and have pulled away from the sides of the tins. Remove from tins right away and place on racks to cool.

PROCEDURE FOR FILLING AND FOR ASSEMBLING CAKE:

1. Place 8 ounces semisweet chocolate in a glass beaker. Cover with plastic, then microwave on high for 1 minute. Cut and stir with a knife, then microwave another minute or until melted and smooth. Add 1 cup cream and whisk until smooth. Add another cup of cream along with ½ cup powdered sugar (measured, then sifted). Whisk to mix, then place uncovered in freezer for 2 hours, stirring halfway through. If the chocolate cream is thick enough so that it does not run, use it. If it is runny, beat it until *barely* thick

enough to use as a cake filling. Do not overbeat. Reserve in refrigerator.

2. Trim tops of cakes level. Cut each into 2 layers. Assemble using ⅓ of the filling in each of the 3 spaces between the 4 layers. As you add each layer, press down to let some of the filling ooze out, then ice the side of the cake with this.

TO ICE AND DECORATE THE TOP:

1. Whip 1 cup cream with 2 tablespoons powdered sugar until stiff but still slightly runny. Ice top of cake only, using part of this cream.

2. Chop 1 ounce semisweet chocolate into pieces and place in a corner of an 11½ × 12½ freezer-weight plastic bag. Tie a knot in the center of the bag. Microwave on high power 1 minute or more, or until chocolate is melted, smooth, and warm. Twist bag to gather chocolate, then make a hole with a round toothpick near the corner where the chocolate is. Have a small knife ready. Holding the bag as if milking a cow, pipe a tight spiral of the warm chocolate on top of the cake. Right away, draw the knife from the center to the outer edge, in 12 evenly spaced strokes around the cake, to get a spiderweb effect.

3. Whip balance of cream stiffer, then pipe decorations on the bottom edge of the cake. Reserve in refrigerator.

TO SERVE: Remove from refrigerator 1 hour before serving.

DO-AHEAD INFORMATION: Cake may be filled, assembled, and kept in refrigerator 1 or 2 days ahead, or it may be frozen and kept for weeks. Finish top 6 to 8 hours before serving.

CHOCOLATE MOUSSE CAKE WITH STRAWBERRIES
(serves 8 to 10)

This chocolate mousse cake is related to one I first heard of about ten years ago. It seems to me I originally saw it in *The New York Times.* It is literally a chocolate mousse put into a baking tin and baked as a cake. To make it moister, the cake is slightly underbaked, but then it sinks in the middle and isn't very pretty. Someone had the bright idea of setting aside some raw mousse, then filling the sunken cake with it later, after the cake had cooled.

For a variation on this chocolate mousse cake, I fold extra chocolate into the filling so that it sets firmer, then I stand strawberries in the mousse, glazing them later with currant jelly. The glistening strawberries and the extra chocolate add a new dimension to this exciting chocolate cake.

INGREDIENTS:

10 ounces semisweet chocolate (total)
1 stick (4 ounces) unsalted butter

8 eggs
½ cup sugar
2 pints strawberries
½ cup red currant jelly

COOKING UTENSIL: An 9-inch springform tin, neither buttered nor floured

PROCEDURE:

1. Preheat oven to 350 degrees.

2. Place 8 ounces semisweet chocolate, broken or chopped, plus butter, sliced, into a 4-cup glass beaker. Cover with plastic, then microwave 2 minutes on high. Cut

and stir with a knife, then microwave 1 minute more, or until chocolate is melted and smooth.

3. Separate eggs, adding yolks to chocolate mixture. Beat at top speed 2 minutes, using a hand-held electric mixer. Reserve.

4. Wash beaters, then add sugar to egg whites and beat at top speed 2 to 3 minutes, or until whites remain in bowl when inverted. Do not overbeat. Transfer whites to a large bowl, then add chocolate mixture and fold with the electric mixer, beating at lowest speed 12 to 15 seconds only, swirling the beaters through the mixture. Finally, fold mixture with a rubber spatula, scraping the bottom of the bowl, using only 8 or 10 strokes.

5. Set aside 1½ cups of the mousse to be used later. Pour the balance into the ungreased baking tin. Bake in preheated 350-degree oven 25–30 minutes. Cake will still be underdone. Remove sides of springform tin, but leave cake on bottom metal disk. Allow to cool on a rack 30 minutes.

6. Place 2 ounces semisweet chocolate, broken or chopped, into a 4-cup glass beaker. Cover with plastic, then microwave on high power 2 minutes, or until melted and smooth. Add the 1½ cups reserved chocolate mousse to the warm chocolate, then carefully but quickly stir or fold together. Pour this into the center of the partially cooled cake and spread evenly. Chill 30 minutes in refrigerator.

7. Brush and hull strawberries, then stand them up in the chocolate. Refrigerate until cake and berries are chilled and mousse is firm. Straighten berries if necessary. Remove metal disk from bottom, then transfer cake to serving plate.

8. Heat currant jelly to boiling, stirring constantly and straining, if necessary, to break up lumps. Brush hot jelly over chilled berries and mousse, adding a tablespoon or two of water if too thick. Refrigerate *uncovered*.

TO SERVE: Serve chilled or bring out to room 30 minutes before serving.

DO-AHEAD INFORMATION. The unglazed cake keeps 1 or 2 days in the refrigerator. Add glaze 6 to 8 hours before serving, then refrigerate uncovered. If cake is covered, glaze melts and runs.

CHOCOLATE MOUSSE LOAF
(serves 8 to 10)

This loaf is a combination of pound-cake slices and chocolate mousse, each slice having an attractive white-and-brown-striped effect. The loaf has a piped whipped-cream decoration and is topped with broken, thin chocolate sheets sprinkled with powdered sugar. It is a lovely and delicious dessert.

INGREDIENTS:

10 ounces semisweet chocolate,* chopped or morsels (total)

1 stick (4 ounces) unsalted butter

3 egg yolks

3 egg whites

3 tablespoons granulated sugar

1 10¾-ounce pound cake,† cut in ⁵⁄₁₆-inch slices

1 cup whipping cream

2 tablespoons powdered sugar + some for dusting

1 teaspoon vanilla

*I used Nestlé's real semisweet chocolate morsels.
†I used Sara Lee All-Butter Pound Cake, but any good pound cake will do. I tried this loaf with chocolate pound cake, but preferred the looks and taste with the white.

SERVING DISH: A serving dish or platter for a 3½ ×
10-inch loaf

PROCEDURE:

1. Place 8 ounces chopped chocolate (or 1½ cups morsels) and 1 stick sliced butter (may be frozen) in a glass
beaker. Microwave 2 minutes on high power, then whisk
until smooth, reheating if necessary. Mixture should be
warm, not hot. Whisk in 3 yolks. Reserve.

2. Mix whites and sugar in a bowl, then beat 2 or 3
minutes at top speed or until stiff enough to stay in bowl
when inverted. Add to chocolate mixture and fold in
thoroughly. Chill 1 or 2 hours, or until firm enough to
spread as a filling.

3. You will use 15 pound-cake slices only. Sandwich
them together in 3 sections of 5 slices each, using 2 to 3
tablespoons chocolate mousse filling between slices. Form
the 5-slice sections, then place them side by side on a
sheet of waxed paper, like three piles of sandwiches, so as
to form a loaf 3½ by 10 inches. (When you cut across loaf
to serve, you will cut across the cake slices.) Ice the top
and sides with any remaining mousse. Wrap waxed paper
around the loaf. Shape into a neat loaf and refrigerate to
set.

4. Place 2 ounces chocolate (about ⅓ cup morsels) in a
glass beaker. Microwave 2 minutes on high power, then stir
until smooth, microwaving another 30 seconds if necessary.
Dump chocolate onto a sheet of waxed paper and spread
with a knife to a rectangle approximately 7 by 8 inches.
Refrigerate.

5. Place loaf on a serving dish or platter. Whip cream,
2 tablespoons powdered sugar, and vanilla until stiff, then
ice the loaf and pipe decorations around the bottom edges

or sides. Peel waxed paper from chocolate, then break into pieces, not too small, and arrange on top of loaf. Dust with powdered sugar. Reserve in refrigerator.

TO SERVE: Serve chilled, as is.

DO-AHEAD INFORMATION: The loaf and the chocolate sheet may be prepared a day ahead. Whip the cream and decorate the loaf 4 or 5 hours before serving. This loaf is perishable; keep refrigerated and eat within 1 or 2 days. The undecorated loaf may be done ahead and frozen, but, because of its perishability, do not keep it, even frozen, for more than 2 weeks.

PECAN TORTE WITH BANANAS

In this dessert cake, spiced pecan layers are brushed with a rum syrup and then put together with a filling of sliced bananas in sweetened whipped cream. The cake is iced and decorated with whipped cream and finished with rows of banana slices in an apricot glaze. This is a beautiful and delicious torte.

INGREDIENTS:

4 eggs
5 ounces pecans
¼ cup all-purpose flour

1 teaspoon baking powder
½ teaspoon cinnamon
Zest of 1 lemon

½ cup sugar (total)

2 teaspoons vanilla (total)

½ cup + 1–2 tablespoons water (total)

2–3 tablespoons dark rum*

1 10-ounce jar apricot jam

2 cups whipping cream

4 tablespoons powdered sugar

4–5 bananas

COOKING UTENSILS: 2 8-inch round cake tins, well buttered, lightly floured

PROCEDURE:

1. Preheat oven to 350 degrees. Warm eggs by placing them, in shells, in a bowl and covering with hot water. Let sit 5 minutes.

2. Place pecans, flour, baking powder, cinnamon, and zest in container of food processor fitted with steel blade. Process 30 seconds, or until nuts are ground fairly fine. Remove to a sheet of waxed paper and reserve.

3. Place eggs and 1 teaspoon vanilla in container of food processor. Pulse 10 to 20 times, then, with the motor running, pour ¼ cup sugar down through feed tube. Stir, then process 30 seconds more. Add reserved nut mixture and process 2 seconds. Stir, then process 2 seconds more. Divide batter into 2 prepared cake tins. Tilt and jiggle to level batter as best you can. Batter will be only about ½-inch high in each pan.

4. Bake in preheated 350-degree oven for 25 to 30 minutes, or until cakes feel firm to the touch and pull away from the sides. Let sit 5 minutes in tins, then unmold onto racks and allow to cool.

*Orange liqueur could be used instead of rum, or apricot brandy or liqueur.

TO ASSEMBLE CAKE:

1. Make a soaking syrup. In a small saucepan put ½ cup water plus ¼ cup sugar. Heat, stirring, just enough to dissolve sugar. Reserve. Just before using, add rum.

2. Place apricot jam in food processor. Process 1 minute, then transfer to a small saucepan. Heat, stirring, until boiling. Stir in 1 or 2 tablespoons water. Allow to cool 20 to 30 minutes, or until barely warm. Mixture must be thick, but still runny enough to be brushed on as a glaze.

3. Whip cream with powdered sugar until stiff but not overbeaten. Slice 2 bananas ³⁄₁₆-inch thick (about 2 cups) and place in a bowl, stirring in 1 cup beaten cream plus 1 teaspoon vanilla. Place 1 cake layer on serving plate. Brush on ½ the rum soaking syrup. Add bananas in cream, pressing until even and level. Add second cake layer. Brush with balance of soaking syrup. Ice top and sides of cake with ¼-inch-thick layer of whipped cream. Slice balance of bananas ³⁄₁₆-inch thick, placing them on a plate. Pour over some of the apricot jam and stir to mix. Place overlapping rows of banana slices on top of cake and spaced out banana slices on cake sides. Brush bananas with additional glaze, then pipe out whipped-cream decorations. Reserve cake in refrigerator.

TO SERVE: Serve chilled. It could be brought out to the room ½ hour before serving so that it is not ice-cold.

DO-AHEAD INFORMATION: Cake layers may be done ahead and frozen. The cake may be completely assembled 6 to 8 hours before serving. Keep refrigerated.

WALNUT TORTE WITH PEACHES AND CREAM
(serves 8 to 10)

This is a wonderful-tasting and elegant dessert torte. Two Viennese-style ground-walnut cake layers are sandwiched together with fresh peaches in sweetened whipped cream and then decorated with whipped cream and chocolate curls. Once the cake layers are made, this is easy, fast, and great.

INGREDIENTS:

4 eggs
6 ounces (2¼ cups)
   shelled walnuts
¼ cup all-purpose flour
½ teaspoon cinnamon
½ cup + 1–2 tablespoons
   granulated sugar
   (total)

2 teaspoons vanilla
3 peaches (1 pound)
2 cups whipping cream
¼ cup powdered sugar
1 ounce semisweet
   chocolate

COOKING UTENSILS: 2 8 × 8 × 2-inch baking tins or 2 8-inch round cake tins; butter and flour the bottoms only, not the sides

PROCEDURE:

1. Preheat oven to 350 degrees. Warm eggs by placing them, in shells, in a bowl and covering with hot water. Let sit 5 minutes.

2. Place walnuts, flour, and cinnamon (no baking powder in this one) in container of food processor fitted with steel blade. Process 20 seconds, or until nuts are ground fairly fine. Transfer to a large bowl and reserve.

3. Place eggs, ½ cup granulated sugar, and vanilla in a small bowl and, using a hand-held electric mixer, beat at top speed for 3 minutes. Moving quickly, dump into nut-flour mixture and fold or stir, using a rubber spatula or a wire whisk. The nuts must be folded in completely, but do not use a single stroke more than necessary, as you must not deflate the eggs. Dump batter into prepared tins.

4. Bake in preheated 350-degree oven 30 minutes, or until cakes have settled (nut cakes rise first, then fall when they are done) and feel firm to the touch. Place in tins on racks. Cut around edges of tins to free cakes, then press down on cake edges to help level the tops. Allow to cool. Turn out on racks. Be careful: they are fragile. Store air-tight until serving time.

5. Wash (or peel, if you like) peaches, then cut into thin, bite-size pieces. Stir in 1 or 2 tablespoons granulated sugar, then refrigerate until time to assemble torte.

6. Place whipping cream and powdered sugar in a bowl and beat until stiff. Choose some attractive peach slices to use as decoration and reserve in refrigerator. Add ½ the whipped cream to the rest of the peach slices and stir to mix.

7. To assemble cake, place 1 layer on a serving dish or platter. Add peaches in cream, then place second layer on top. Frost top and sides with remaining whipped cream.

8. Warm chocolate 15 to 30 seconds in microwave and scrape curls, using a vegetable peeler. Reserve in refrigerator until serving time.

TO SERVE: Add peach slices and chocolate curls and serve chilled, as is. For the square cake, divide it in half, then cut halves across into 1½-inch slices.

DO-AHEAD INFORMATION: The cake layers, wrapped in plastic, will keep several days in the room. They may also be frozen. Slice peaches 5 or 6 hours ahead and assemble the cake 3 to 4 hours before serving. Keep refrigerated.

9

SPECTACULAR LIGHT CAKE DESSERTS

SPONGECAKE BASES
BUTTER SPONGECAKE TART SHELL
BASIC BUTTER SPONGECAKE LAYERS
CHOCOLATE BUTTER SPONGECAKE

THE CAKES
APRICOT CAKE-TART
PINEAPPLE-COCONUT CAKE-TART
RASPBERRY-APPLESAUCE CAKE-TART
TANGERINE CAKE-TART
CARAMEL PECAN SURPRISE CAKE
CHOCOLATE-COATED PEAR CAKE
LIME MERINGUE CAKE
STRAWBERRY TAJ MAHAL

The recipes in this chapter fit into the category of pastries that some people are calling *nouvelle pâtisserie,* or New Pastry. This is a recent movement toward pastries that are lighter in looks and texture and supposedly in calories. The desserts are generally airier and lighter, with sponge layers of instead of *génoises* and fillings and frostings of fruits and whipped cream instead of buttercream and fondant. There is a serious attempt in the New Pastry to use less fat and less sugar.

The eight desserts in this chapter are light in texture and feeling. Four of them are what I call cake-tarts. They were discovered accidentally one day when my spongecakes fell. As I was looking at these awful, sunken things, suddenly I thought of filling them with fruit. Well, they work great and you will really like the cake-tarts. They are refreshing, delicious, and truly a little lower in calories than most desserts that look and taste this good.

The other four cakes in this chapter are spongecakes that are split, filled, and decorated. They are all really good and really beautiful, and one of them, the Strawberry Taj Mahal, is probably the prettiest dessert in the book.

My favorites in this chapter, in order of preference, are: Strawberry Taj Mahal, Chocolate-Coated Pear Cake, Raspberry-Applesauce Cake-Tart, and Pineapple-Coconut Cake-Tart.

The chapter starts off with the three cake bases that the light desserts use: a spongecake shell for the four cake-tarts, and basic butter and chocolate spongecakes for the others.

BUTTER SPONGECAKE TART SHELL
(makes 2 9-inch shells)

This recipe makes 2 low spongecakes that become delicious bases for fruit fillings and toppings. The 4 cake-tarts in this chapter that use these bases are among the nicest, most refreshing, and most beautiful desserts in the book. If by chance your cakes should collapse in the center, which has occasionally happened to me, don't despair, but congratulate yourself because you will have even better tartlike shapes with which to complete your desserts.

INGREDIENTS:

1 stick (4 ounces) unsalted butter
1 cup cake flour
1 teaspoon baking powder
6 eggs

Zest of one lemon
1 tablespoon lemon juice
1 teaspoon vanilla
1 cup sugar

COOKING UTENSILS: 2 9-inch springform tins, prepared as described below

PROCEDURE:

1. Preheat oven to 350 degrees. Slice butter and melt. Spoon 1 teaspoon melted butter into each of the springform tins. Smear around bottoms of tins only, *not sides.* Flour tin bottoms lightly and tap out.

2. Sift flour once or twice, then mix in sifter with baking powder and reserve.

3. Separate eggs, placing yolks in a large mixing bowl and whites in a smaller, deep one. To the yolks, add zest, lemon juice, and vanilla. Stir and reserve.

4. Reheat butter until bubbly around the edges. Reserve. Add sugar to the egg whites; then, using the hand-held electric mixer, beat at highest speed, swirling beaters all the time. Beat 5 or 6 minutes or until whites stay in inverted bowl. Do not overbeat.

5. Right away, dump whites on top of yolks in the large bowl. Sift flour mixture over the whites, then quickly dribble the warm butter over the flour. Using the hand-held electric mixer, fold by beating mixture at lowest speed, swirling the beaters broadly in the batter for 15 to 20 seconds, or until batter looks fairly smooth. Finally, using a rubber spatula, stir or fold, using 8 or 10 strokes only, scraping the bottom and sides of the bowl to make sure the butter and flour are incorporated. Don't be concerned if batter is slightly lumpy from the flour.

6. Right away, pour equal amounts of batter into the 2 tins. Tilt to level, letting batter run up edges of tins a good ½ inch or so. Bake in preheated 350-degree oven 25 to 30 minutes, or until nicely browned. Allow to cool in tins, on racks. Important: Do not remove from tins and do not cut cakes from sides. You are going to pour liquid fillings into these shells, and cakes must be still stuck to the sides so that

the fillings do not run down the cracks. Chill or freeze cakes in tins.

DO-AHEAD INFORMATION: Cakes may be frozen and kept 1 or 2 weeks.

BASIC BUTTER SPONGECAKE LAYERS
(makes 2 8 ½-inch layers)

Please read the section on Hints for No-Fail Cake Making in the Introduction to the book. It was written with this recipe especially in mind.

INGREDIENTS:

1 stick (4 ounces) unsalted butter
1½ cups cake flour
1 teaspoon baking powder
8 eggs

Zest of one lemon
1 tablespoon lemon juice
1 teaspoon vanilla
1¼ cups sugar (total)

COOKING UTENSILS: 2 9-inch springform pans, prepared per instructions below

PROCEDURE:

1. Preheat oven to 350 degrees. Slice butter, then melt in a small saucepan. Place 2 teaspoons melted butter in each of the 2 springform pans. Smear butter on bottom and sides of pans, then flour the tins, tapping out excess. Reserve balance of melted butter.

2. Fluff flour into cups to measure, then sift once or twice. Return to sifter mixed with the baking powder. Reserve.

3. Separate eggs, placing yolks in a 4-cup bowl and whites in a 6-cup bowl. To the yolks add zest, lemon juice, vanilla, and ¾ cup sugar. Mix *right away;* then, using a hand-held electric mixer, beat at highest speed 2 minutes or until mixture is pale and frothy but not stiff. Do not overbeat. Transfer to a large bowl for folding. Reserve.

4. Reheat butter until bubbly around the edges. Reserve.

5. Wash beaters, then add ½ cup sugar to the whites and beat at highest speed, swirling beaters all the time, 4 to 5 minutes or until whites stay in bowl when held upside down. Do not overbeat.

6. Right away, dump whites on top of yolks. Sift the flour over the whites, then quickly dribble the warm butter over the flour. Using the electric mixer, fold by beating mixture at lowest speed, swirling the beaters broadly in the batter for 15 to 20 seconds only, or until batter looks fairly smooth. Finally, using a rubber spatula, stir or fold in 8 or 10 strokes only, scraping the bottom and sides of the bowl to make sure the butter and flour are incorporated. Don't be concerned if batter is slightly lumpy from the flour.

7. Right away, pour equal amounts of batter into the 2 prepared tins. Tilt to level, then bake in preheated 350-degree oven 30 minutes or until nicely browned. Remove cakes from tins right away and allow to cool on racks.

DO-AHEAD INFORMATION: Cakes may be done ahead and kept frozen for several weeks.

CHOCOLATE BUTTER SPONGECAKE
(makes 2 cakes)

This recipe is the same as the Basic Butter Spongecake Layers except that ½ cup cocoa is substituted for ½ cup of the flour. There are a few other minor changes, but the ingredients and procedure are essentially the same. This batch yields one 8-inch square cake (used for the Strawberry Taj Mahal) and one 8-inch round cake that you may freeze and use another time. Try using it for a chocolate version of the Caramel Pecan Surprise Cake or for the Chocolate-Coated Pear Cake, or make up your own combination.

INGREDIENTS:

1 stick (4 ounces) unsalted butter	1 teaspoon baking powder
1 cup cake flour	8 eggs
½ cup cocoa	1¼ cups sugar (total)
	1 teaspoon vanilla

COOKING UTENSILS: 2 8-inch-square cake tins with 2-inch-high sides; or 1 8-inch springform tin and 1 8-inch-square cake tin

PROCEDURE:

1. Preheat oven to 350 degrees. Slice butter, then melt in a small saucepan. Place 2 teaspoons melted butter in each of the 2 cake tins. Smear butter on bottom and sides of pans, then flour the tins, tapping out excess. Reserve balance of melted butter.

2. Fluff flour and cocoa into cups to measure, then sift once or twice with baking powder and finally return mixture to sifter. Reserve.

3. Separate eggs, placing yolks in a 4-cup bowl and

whites in a 6-cup bowl. Add ¾ cup sugar plus vanilla to the yolks and mix *right away.* Using a hand-held electric mixer, beat at highest speed 2 minutes, or until mixture is pale and frothy but not stiff. Do not overbeat. Transfer to a large bowl and reserve.

4. Reheat butter until bubbly around the edges. Reserve. Wash beaters, then add ½ cup sugar to whites and beat at highest speed, swirling beater all the time, 4 to 5 minutes, or until whites stay in bowl when held upside down. Do not overbeat.

5. Right away, dump whites on top of yolks. Sift the flour mixture over the whites. Quickly dribble the warm butter over the flour; then, using the electric mixer, fold by beating mixture at lowest speed, swirling the beaters broadly in the batter for 15 to 20 seconds only, or until batter looks fairly smooth. Finally, using a rubber spatula, stir or fold in 10 to 12 strokes only, scraping the bottom and sides of the bowl to make sure butter and flour are incorporated. Don't be concerned if batter is slightly lumpy from the flour.

6. Pour batter into square tin to fill ⅔ full. Pour balance of batter into springform tin. Tilt to level, then bake in preheated 350-degree oven 25 to 30 minutes, or until cakes have shrunk from sides of tin and a toothpick inserted in center comes out clean. Remove cakes from tins right away and allow to cool on racks.

DO-AHEAD INFORMATION: Cakes may be done ahead and kept frozen for several weeks.

APRICOT CAKE-TART
(serves 6 to 8)

This lovely, light, and delicious sponge cake-tart is filled with sweetened, jellied, puréed apricots; then apricot halves are embedded in the purée and their depressions filled with candied cherries that have soaked in rum. The colors of the apricots and cherries are so pretty by themselves that this tart doesn't need any whipped-cream decorations.

INGREDIENTS:
20 candied cherries (about 4 ounces)
2 tablespoons rum (optional: additional 2 tablespoons for sprinkling cake)
1 Butter Spongecake Tart Shell

2 17-ounce cans unpeeled apricot halves in syrup
1 rounded teaspoon plain gelatin
2 tablespoons sugar (or more, to taste)

SERVING DISH: A silver platter or attractive cake plate

PROCEDURE:
1. Place candied cherries in a small dish and add 2 tablespoons rum. Let marinate for 1 or 2 hours or longer.
2. Have spongecake shell chilled, still attached to the sides of the springform tin. Drain contents of 2 cans of apricots, reserving syrup. Choose 18 to 20 pretty apricot halves (depending upon size) to occupy most of the area on the top of the cake. Place balance (about ¾ cup, packed down tight) in food processor fitted with steel blade. Process to a smooth purée. Reserve.

3. Into a 4-quart glass beaker put 2 tablespoons reserved syrup from cans. Sprinkle over gelatin and let soften 2 minutes. Microwave on high power for 30 seconds, or until boiling, then add sugar and stir to dissolve. Add ¼ cup apricot purée and stir to mix, then add this mixture to the apricot purée and process to mix.

4. Sprinkle 2 tablespoons rum over spongecake shell, if you wish, then pour in apricot purée. Arrange apricot halves, hole sides up, in an attractive pattern. Refrigerate until set. Place a marinated candied cherry in the center hole of each apricot half. When set, neatly cut cake out of tin and place on serving dish. Reserve in refrigerator.

TO SERVE: Serve chilled, or bring out to room ½ hour before serving. Serve as is, or accompanied by sweetened, flavored whipped cream.

DO-AHEAD INFORMATION: The spongecake shell may be done ahead and frozen. The cake may be assembled a day or two ahead and stored, covered with plastic, in the refrigerator.

PINEAPPLE-COCONUT CAKE-TART
(serves 8)

The combination of pineapple and coconut in this cake-tart makes this dessert a natural to top off a meal with a tropical theme. Served chilled, this dessert is refreshing, slightly tart, and quite delicious. If the décor scares you, instead of the 9 circles on the top, spread the crushed pineapple in one large area in the center, piping whipped cream around the edges.

INGREDIENTS:

1 Butter Spongecake Tart Shell

1 20-ounce can crushed pineapple, in heavy syrup

3 rounded teaspoons plain gelatin

3–4 tablespoons granulated sugar

2 cups unsweetened pineapple juice (total)

1 cup (3½ ounces) sweetened shredded or flaked coconut

3 tablespoons puréed apricot preserves*

1 cup whipping cream

2 tablespoons powdered sugar

SERVING DISH: A silver platter or attractive cake plate

PROCEDURE:

1. Have cake shell chilled. Drain crushed pineapple, reserving syrup. Measure 1 cup crushed pineapple and set aside for décor. Arrange balance of crushed pineapple (approximately ¾ cup) in spongecake shell in an even layer. Reserve.

2. Place 3 tablespoons syrup from crushed pineapple into a 4-cup glass beaker. Sprinkle gelatin over and whisk to mix. Let soften 1 minute. Microwave on high power 30 to 60 seconds, or until boiling. Add granulated sugar and stir to dissolve. Add ½ cup unsweetened pineapple juice. Stir to mix, heating if necessary if mixture is not smooth. Reserve.

3. Place coconut in container of food processor fitted

*Buy an 18-ounce jar of apricot jam or preserves; process contents until fairly smooth. Stir in 1 tablespoon water, then return to jar and store in refrigerator to use as needed.

with steel blade. Process 1 minute, stirring down once or twice. Add ¼ cup unsweetened pineapple juice and process 30 seconds. Add another ¼ cup and process again. Continue adding pineapple juice until a total of 1½ cups have been added. Add gelatin mixture* and process to mix. Pour into spongecake shell. Chill, level, in refrigerator 1 or 2 hours or until set.

4. Neatly cut cake out of tin and place on serving dish. Stir puréed apricot preserves into reserved cup of crushed pineapple. Whip cream and powdered sugar until stiff. Pipe out 8 circles 2¼ inches in diameter around the outer top edge of the cake and one 3¼-inch circle in the center. Fill circles with crushed pineapple-apricot mixture, then pipe tiny rosettes over the whipped-cream circles. Refrigerate.

TO SERVE: Serve chilled, or remove from refrigerator ½ hour ahead so that it is not ice-cold.

DO-AHEAD INFORMATION: The spongecake shell may be done 1 or 2 weeks ahead and frozen. The filling may be added 1 or 2 days ahead. Add whipped cream and crushed pineapple 4 or 5 hours before serving.

RASPBERRY-APPLESAUCE CAKE-TART
(serves 8)

Here's the winner of the four cake-tarts as far as I'm concerned. This one is filled with a layer of jellied applesauce and apple juice plus an additional layer of raspberries in a

*If gelatin mixture has set, reheat just until liquid again.

beautiful, clear red jelly made of the syrup from the raspberries. It is then decorated with whipped cream. This is a
very delicious, exciting, and glamorous dessert.

INGREDIENTS:

1 Butter Spongecake Tart
    Shell
1 16-ounce can applesauce
1½ cups (about) pure
    apple juice* (total)
6 level teaspoons plain
    gelatin (total)

3 10-ounce packages
    frozen red raspberries,
    packed with sugar
    and water, defrosted
1 cup whipping cream
2 tablespoons powdered
    sugar

SERVING DISH: A silver platter or attractive cake plate

PROCEDURE:

1. Have cake shell chilled, still attached to the sides of
the springform tin. Place applesauce in a 4-cup measure,
then add enough apple juice to make a total of 3 cups of
mixture. Stir to mix. Have at room temperature.

2. Place 3 tablespoons apple juice in a 1-quart glass
beaker. Sprinkle 3 level teaspoons plain gelatin on top and
whisk to mix. Let soften 2 minutes. Microwave, uncovered,
on high power 30 to 60 seconds, or until boiling hot. Stir
well, then add ½ cup applesauce mixture. Mix again, then
add gelatin mixture to balance of applesauce mixture.
Whisk well, then pour into cake shell. Place level in freezer
and let chill 40 minutes, or until set.

3. Drain raspberries, reserving syrup (approximately 2
cups†). Place 3 tablespoons raspberry syrup in a 1-quart
glass beaker. Sprinkle balance of 3 level teaspoons of gelatin

*It may be either clear or cloudy as you like.
†Add water if needed to get 2 cups.

on top. Stir, then allow to soften 3 or 4 minutes. Place drained raspberries in a single layer over jellied applesauce. Microwave gelatin mixture on full power, uncovered, 30 to 60 seconds, or until boiling hot. Stir, then add ¼ cup raspberry syrup and stir to mix, being careful not to cause bubbles. Stir in balance of raspberry syrup. Carefully pour over raspberries in springform tin. Place level in refrigerator. If necessary, press raspberries down a bit with a fork to help submerge in the liquid. Chill several hours, or until set.

4. Cut cake neatly out of tin and place on serving platter. Whip cream with powdered sugar, then pipe vertical streaks of whipped cream (I used Ateco tip 6-B) from base of dessert to the top to completely cover the sides. The French call this decoration *flammes.* Leave the pretty red top untouched.

TO SERVE: Serve chilled. The raspberry top has just enough gelatin in it to barely hold. If you have to hold this dessert awhile in a warm room, you should double the amount of gelatin in the raspberry mixture.

DO-AHEAD INFORMATION: The spongecake shell may be done 2 weeks or more ahead and frozen. Fillings may be added 1 or 2 days ahead and the dessert stored in the refrigerator. Add whipped-cream decoration 4 or 5 hours before serving.

TANGERINE CAKE-TART
(serves 8)

The colors of this orange-on-orange cake-tart are beautiful. Fresh tangerines, cut and mixed with slightly sweetened tangerine juice and a little gelatin, fill the hollow of the cake. It is then decorated with fresh tangerine slices, with a tiny rosette of whipped cream in the center of each one. This is so fresh and wholesome, you could have a slice of it for breakfast. It's the egg, toast, butter, and orange juice all wrapped up in one.

INGREDIENTS:

1 Butter Spongecake Tart Shell

4 pounds tangerines (12 large ones, if possible)

1 envelope plain gelatin

2 tablespoons granulated sugar

1 cup whipping cream

2 tablespoons powdered sugar

SERVING DISH: A silver platter or attractive cake plate

PROCEDURE:

1. Have cake shell chilled, still attached to the sides of the springform tin. Divide tangerines into 3 groups. In the first group, place 4 equal-size tangerines to be sliced with skins for decoration. In the second group, put aside 2 or 3 to be squeezed for juice. The third group will consist of the balance of the tangerines, which will be cut and used as tangerine pieces.

2. Of the third group of tangerines, grate zest from 2 of them and place in a 4-cup measure (this is optional). Peel all the tangerines in this third group and pull them apart into sections. Using a sharp knife, cut across the thin, angled

section of each segment (the part that used to be at the center of the tangerine), removing and discarding a strip of the toughest part of the membrane and opening up the segment. Scrape out seeds, then cut segments across into 3 or 4 pieces. Place in 4-cup measure.

3. Squeeze juice from 2 or 3 reserved tangerines (this was group 2), adding it to tangerine pieces. You should have a total of approximately 2⅔ cups. Reserve.

4. Into a 4-cup glass beaker place 3 tablespoons of the tangerine juice you just squeezed. Sprinkle gelatin over this and whisk to mix. Let soften 1 minute, then microwave on full power 30 to 60 seconds or until boiling hot. Add granulated sugar and whisk well to dissolve sugar. Add ¼ cup tangerine pulp-liquid to gelatin mixture, stirring well to mix. Add the rest of the pulp-liquid and mix well again. Pour into cake shell, pressing down with a rubber spatula to level. Chill several hours in refrigerator, or until set.

5. Using a sharp knife, cutting through skin and flesh, cut off and discard the tops and bottoms of the 4 tangerines from group 1, cutting off pieces about ⅜-inch thick. Next cut 1 or 2 even, perfect ⅛-inch-thick slices from the cut ends of each tangerine. You need 9 slices altogether. By using slices close to the ends of the tangerines, with luck, you will have perfect slices with no seeds. Reserve.

6. Cut cake neatly out of tin and place on serving dish. Place 8 tangerine slices around top edge and 1 in the center. Refrigerate, covered with plastic.

7. Whip cream with powdered sugar until stiff. Reserve in refrigerator. Before serving, pipe a small rosette (I used tip 3-B) in the center of each tangerine slice.

TO SERVE: Serve chilled, or remove from refrigerator ½ hour before serving. Serve balance of whipped cream on side (optional), stirring in a little orange (or tangerine) liqueur or vanilla, if you like.

DO-AHEAD INFORMATION: The spongecake shell may be done ahead and frozen. It may be filled and the tangerine slices cut and placed on top 1 or 2 days ahead. Keep refrigerated, covered with plastic. Whipped-cream decorations may be added 3 or 4 hours before serving, and the tart left uncovered in the refrigerator until serving time.

CARAMEL PECAN SURPRISE CAKE
(serves 8)

This starts with a spongecake that is split, filled, and glazed with apricot jam. Then the whole is iced with whipped cream and streaked with an easy chocolate grid. The surprise in this wonderful cake is the caramel-pecan layer that you can't see because it's on the bottom. It is pretty enough to be on the top, but if it were there, your fork would never get through it and you wouldn't be able to eat the cake.

I think of this cake as reverse chic—somewhat like a cloth coat lined with sable.

INGREDIENTS:

1 8½-inch Basic Butter
   Spongecake Layer
3 ounces pecans (½ cup
   halves), ¼-inch dice
½ stick (2 ounces)
   unsalted butter

¼ cup granulated sugar
1 rounded tablespoon
   white Karo
2 tablespoons whipping
   cream
2 teaspoons vanilla (total)

⅓ cup apricot jam or
preserves*
1 cup whipping cream

2 tablespoons powdered
sugar
1 ounce semisweet
chocolate

COOKING UTENSIL AND SERVING DISH: A baking sheet
and a silver platter or attractive cake plate

PROCEDURE:

1. Preheat oven to 375 degrees. Place oven shelf so
nut-caramel (see step 3) can bake in upper third. Cut the
spongecake sideways into 3 layers. Place the bottom half,
bottom up, on a baking sheet. Reserve.

2. Have chopped pecans ready and waiting on the side.
Place butter, granulated sugar, Karo, and whipping cream in
a 1½-quart saucepan. Bring to a boil over medium heat,
stirring most of the time to help dissolve the sugar. When
boil is reached and sugar is dissolved, turn heat to high and
cook *exactly* 2 minutes, not stirring anymore. The mixture
should just be starting to color a light brown. Right away,
add pecans plus 1 teaspoon vanilla. Stir with a spoon, then
dump out onto cake bottom. Using a fork, spread nuts into
an even layer on the cake.

3. Bake in upper third of preheated 375-degree oven for
10 minutes, or until caramel mixture is bubbly all over.
Remove from oven and allow to cool an hour or more on a
rack.

4. Turn cake over and spread with a thin layer of apricot jam. Place center cake layer over, then spread with apricot and cover it with top layer. Press to re-form cake. Trans-

*Buy a 10-ounce jar of apricot jam or preserves. Place contents in food
processor and process 1 or 2 minutes, or until lumps are pretty well
gone. Stir in 1 tablespoon water. Return to jar and allow to cool. Cover
and store in refrigerator.

fer cake to serving dish, keeping nut side down. Refrigerate until chilled.

5. Whip cream with powdered sugar and 1 teaspoon vanilla, then ice top and sides of cake, using all the cream. Place semisweet chocolate in a corner of an 11½ × 12½-inch freezer-weight plastic bag.* Tie a knot in the center of the bag. Microwave on high power 1½ minutes, then knead chocolate to break up lumps. Microwave another 30 seconds, or until chocolate is melted and quite warm. Twist the bag to get the chocolate together, then poke a round toothpick into the bag near corner where chocolate is. Drive it in about 1 inch, then remove. Holding the bag as if milking a cow, streak the top of the cake with chocolate going in one direction, then rotate cake 90 degrees and streak again to get a grid pattern. Lift the cake, tilting a bit, then streak the sides. Refrigerate.

TO SERVE: Serve chilled, or remove from refrigerator 1 hour before serving. When serving, press hard to cut through the nut layer on the bottom.

DO-AHEAD INFORMATION: Cake may be baked, assembled with apricot jam, then frozen for 3 or more weeks. Whipped cream and chocolate grid may be added 1 or 2 days ahead. Cover cake with plastic and keep refrigerated.

CHOCOLATE-COATED PEAR CAKE
(serves 8)

This is one of the best-loved desserts in the book—once again, it's the magical combination of pears and chocolate

*I use Glad food storage bags.

that does it. I've served it with two or three other desserts from this book at several dinners and it has always come out first. People love it. It's very clean-tasting and simple and very easy once you have made the no-fail spongecake layers.

INGREDIENTS:

1 Basic Butter Spongecake Layer

¾ cup apricot jam or preserves

1 tablespoon water

2 16-ounce cans Bartlett pear halves

8 ounces semisweet chocolate

1 stick (4 ounces) unsalted butter

2 tablespoons white Karo (or honey)

1 cup whipping cream

2 tablespoons powdered sugar

1 teaspoon vanilla

SERVING DISH: A silver platter or attractive cake plate

PROCEDURE:

1. Split the spongecake into 3 layers, using the thread technique described in the Hints for No-Fail Cake Making section in the book's Introduction.

2. Place jam in processor fitted with steel blade and process to a smooth purée. Stir in 1 tablespoon water, then spread jam between cake layers. You may use less than ¾ cup jam, but don't be too stingy with it. Reassemble cake and place on serving dish.

3. Drain pear halves, then select 8 of the prettiest and arrange in a ring on the top of the cake, placing the narrow sections of the pears toward the center. Round off one of the leftover pears with a knife, then fit this piece in the center. Blot pears dry with a towel.

4. Break or chop the chocolate a little and slice butter into pieces. Place these in a 1-quart glass beaker, adding the

Karo. Cover with plastic and microwave 1½ minutes. Stir with a spatula, avoiding creating bubbles, until mixture is shiny and smooth. Reheat 30 to 60 seconds in microwave, if necessary, or until mixture is very warm. It must not be too hot, however, or the fat may separate out of the chocolate on cooling.

5. Place cake on a rack over a clean baking sheet to catch the drippings. Pour warm coating over pears, concentrating on getting pears coated completely.* You may use all the chocolate to coat the pears and the top of the cake. When all the coating has been poured, pick up the cake on the rack and, holding the sides of the cake, tilt to smooth the coating and to aim excess so that it coats the sides of the cake. The top should be perfect; you should not have to touch it again, but you may touch up the sides. Using a knife, scrape chocolate from the baking sheet and fix any missing side areas. Refrigerate until set, then cut carefully from rack and place on serving dish.

6. Whip cream with powdered sugar and vanilla. Reserve in refrigerator. Three or 4 hours before serving, pipe rosettes of cream on the cake.

TO SERVE: This cake tastes better at room temperature and not chilled, so bring it out of refrigerator at least 1 hour before serving. In warming, the chocolate will also regain some of its shine. Pass balance of whipped cream around at the table.

DO-AHEAD INFORMATION: Cake layers may be done ahead and kept in freezer for several weeks. Cake may be assem-

*There is more coating than you will need so that you will have plenty to pour over the pears. Let excess run off and when it has cooled to the right consistency, roll into balls and eat as chocolate truffles.

bled and coated with chocolate 1 or 2 days ahead and kept in refrigerator. Once chocolate is set, cover with plastic. Whipped-cream decorations may be added 4 or 5 hours before serving.

LIME MERINGUE CAKE
(serves 8)

Here is a fresh and delightful cake dessert, another lovely and delicious use for the Basic Butter Spongecake Layers. Two layers of lime* filling are combined with two cake layers, then a glamorous meringue is piped on top. The lime filling is a simple variation of classic French pastry cream, using limeade instead of milk. The meringue top is piped out with a pastry bag and looks lovely, but if piping scares you, you may spread the meringue with a knife. The cake may not look quite so fabulous, but it will still be very nice.

INGREDIENTS:

1 Basic Butter Spongcake
    Layer
3 eggs
½ + ⅜ cup granulated
    sugar (total)
2½ tablespoons flour
Zest of 2 limes

3–4 tablespoons lime juice
1 cup water
2+ tablespoons unsalted
    butter
1 tablespoon powdered
    sugar

COOKING UTENSIL AND SERVING DISH: A baking sheet and a silver platter or attractive cake plate

*If you can't find limes, you may substitute lemons for this.

PROCEDURE:

1. Separate eggs. Place whites in a small mixing bowl and reserve. Place the 3 yolks in a 1½-quart saucepan. Add ½ cup granulated sugar and stir to mix. Mix in flour, then stir in lime zest and juice plus water.

2. Bring yolk mixture to a boil over high heat, whisking all the time once mixture starts to get hot. Lower heat and allow to simmer 2 minutes. Off heat, whisk in butter, cut in pieces. Spread mixture on a dinner plate. Touch a piece of butter all over the top surface of the mixture (to prevent a skin), then place in freezer for 30 to 60 minutes, or until chilled and set. Store in refrigerator.

3. Preheat oven to 425 degrees. Cut spongecake in half to make 2 layers. Place bottom layer on a baking sheet. Mix the lime cream with a rubber spatula to make it spreadable (do not whisk), then spread ½ over the cake layer. Place top layer over, then spread balance of lime cream on the top, keeping it slightly away from the outside top edge.

4. Add ⅜ cup granulated sugar to reserved egg whites, then beat to inverted-bowl stage. Spread sides of cake with thin layer of meringue, then pipe meringue rosettes in a solid layer on top of the cake (I used Ateco tip 6-B), making sure rosettes are in contact with each other and anchored all around to meringued sides of the cake. Sieve powdered sugar lightly over the top.

5. Place cake in preheated 425-degree oven and bake 8 or 9 minutes, or until meringue is lightly browned. Allow to cool, then transfer to serving plate and refrigerate.

TO SERVE: Serve chilled, or remove from refrigerator 1 hour before serving.

DO-AHEAD INFORMATION: Cake may be made and assembled with the lime cream, then frozen for several weeks. Add and bake meringue 1 or 2 days before serving. Keep refrigerated.

STRAWBERRY TAJ MAHAL
(serves 8 to 10)

This three-tiered chocolate cake is truly spectacular and lovely. A Chocolate Butter Spongecake is split, spread with strawberry jam, then topped with sliced strawberries in whipped cream. The cake is iced with whipped cream, the sides decorated with rows of strawberry slices, and the top covered with chocolate sheets. A crushed strawberry sauce is served alongside. This is obviously not a 15-minute dessert, but considering its beauty and complexity, it is amazingly fast. If you get really good strawberries to use in it, you will not find a lovelier, more delicious dessert in this book.

INGREDIENTS:

1 8-inch-square Chocolate Butter Spongecake
1 cup strawberry jam (or less)
1 cup whipping cream
2 tablespoons powdered sugar, plus extra
3 pints strawberries
1–2 tablespoons granulated sugar
2 ounces semisweet chocolate

SERVING DISH: A silver platter or attractive cake plate

PROCEDURE:

1. Split cake into 3 layers, using the thread technique described in the Hints for No-Fail Cake Making section in the book's Introduction.

2. Place jam in processor fitted with steel blade and process to a smooth purée. Spread jam between the layers (don't be too stingy), then reassemble and place on serving dish. (Optional: spread jam on top and sides of cake.)

3. Whip cream with 2 tablespoons powdered sugar until stiff. Reserve in refrigerator.

4. Brush or wipe strawberries and hull them. Slice into ⅛-inch slices, going from top to bottom. Set aside 48 of the prettiest and most symmetrical slices for the final décor and reserve in refrigerator.

4. Place 3 cups of the remaining sliced berries in a mixing bowl and reserve. These will be mixed with whipped cream and used on top of the cake.

5. Place balance of strawberries in food processor and add 1 or 2 tablespoons granulated sugar. Process to a runny, lumpy sauce consistency. Reserve in refrigerator until serving time.

6. Fold ½ cup of the reserved, sweetened whipped cream into the 3 cups of reserved, sliced berries. Taste and add more sugar if desired. Dump out on top of the cake. Shape berries into a flat, even layer, slightly smaller than the bottom one, allowing a ledge about ½ inch wide on all 4 sides of the cake.

7. Ice the sides of the cake and the ledges with the balance of the whipped cream. Do not ice the top. Embed the reserved, neat strawberry slices, standing up in rows, in the cream on the sides around both the bottom and the top layers. Reserve cake in refrigerator.

8. Break up chocolate and place in 4-cup glass beaker.

Cover and microwave on high for 1 minute. Cut and stir, microwaving another 30 to 60 seconds, if necessary, or until melted and smooth. Using an icing spreader, spread chocolate in a rectangle, approximately 9 × 14 inches, on a sheet of waxed paper. Place in refrigerator so that it is not lying flat but is curved a bit. I drape it over a couple of wine bottles lying separated on their sides.

8. In 30 minutes or more, when chocolate has set, peel paper from the back, then break chocolate into irregular pieces, roughly 3 × 4 inches. Place on a dish and return immediately to refrigerator.

9. Arrange chocolate sheets on top of cake so that they cover the area and look good. Sprinkle a light coating of powdered sugar through a sieve over the chocolate.

TO SERVE: Serve chilled, or let cake sit out 30 minutes before serving. The best way to cut the cake is to first divide it in half, then slice each half across into servings 1 to 1½ inches thick, or as you like. Spoon sauce over each cake slice.

DO-AHEAD INFORMATION: The spongecake may be made weeks ahead and frozen. You may slice berries, completely assemble cake, and prepare sauce 5 or 6 hours before serving. Keep refrigerated, covered with plastic.

10

ICE CREAMS AND FROZEN DESSERTS

COUPES

APRICOT–BING CHERRY COUPE

BLUEBERRY COUPE

COFFEE–CHOCOLATE COUPE

TOASTED HAZELNUT COUPE

LEMON COUPE WITH CANDIED PEEL

MAPLE PECAN COUPE

PEARS IN SPICED RED WINE COUPE

PECAN BALLS WITH BROWN SUGAR SAUCE

RASPBERRY COUPE WITH GRAND MARNIER

FANCY ICE-CREAM DESSERTS

FROZEN CHOCOLATE SQUARES

CHOCOLATE TOASTED-ALMOND ICE-CREAM BOMBE

FLEUR–DE–LYS

STRAWBERRY–BANANA ICE–CREAM RING

People love ice-cream desserts and I think your guests will be thrilled with all the desserts in this chapter. Probably the loveliest and easiest dessert in this book is to be found here. It is a four-flavored ice-cream dish called Fleur-de-Lys, and you won't find a faster and more fabulous dessert anywhere.

My personal favorites of the coupes in this chapter are the Blueberry, the Raspberry with Grand Marnier, and the Apricot–Bing Cherry coupes. I love the four fancy ice-cream desserts almost equally well, but my slight order of preference is Fleur-de-Lys, Strawberry-Banana Ring, Chocolate Toasted-Almond Bombe, and Frozen Chocolate Squares. Something tells me, however, that the average person will probably prefer these desserts in exactly the reverse order.

SOME IMPORTANT NOTES ON
COMMERCIAL ICE CREAMS

Many of the desserts in this chapter are based on commercial ice creams. Here are some very important notes about them.

1. In this chapter, when a recipe calls for 1 quart of ice cream, that means 1 quart of *hand-packed* ice cream. If you buy machine-packed, you must buy 2 quarts (a half gallon) to get the same amount. Machine-packed ice cream is full of air. As you stir things into it, you will notice that the half gallon of ice cream packs down to 1 quart.

2. Judge commercial ice creams by flavor, not by richness. The most important thing in ice cream is not the amount of heavy cream it contains but the amount of real fruit, chocolate, nuts, raisins, coffee, real vanilla, etc., used in it.

3. Try to find ice cream that contains no artificial color. This may be difficult, but give it a try. The awful colors used in the sherbets bother me the most. The artificial yellow, green, and orange colors used in lemon, lime, and orange sherbets frequently have no relationship at all to the true colors of the natural juices. It makes you wonder if the products contain any real fruit at all.

4. If you search for bargain prices in ice creams, you will probably end up with a poor-quality product. One of the best ice creams available in San Francisco is called Double Rainbow. As of March 1984, the price for 2 pounds of their *hand-packed* ice cream (equivalent to 1 quart) was $5.25. The same week, at a supermarket, I bought a half gallon (2 quarts by volume) of *machine-packed* ice cream. It was a well-advertised local brand, generally considered fairly good quality. The price for the half gallon was $3.99. "Good-

ness," said I to myself, "that Double Rainbow stuff is expensive. It costs considerably more than double the price of the other one."

At home I weighed the *1 quart* of hand-packed Double Rainbow and found that it weighed exactly the same as the machine-packed *2 quarts* from the supermarket. Ounce by ounce, the fine-quality ice cream cost only 30 percent more and it was well worth it. You had only to look at the difference in color of the two chocolate ice creams to realize the difference in the quality of the two brands.

APRICOT–BING CHERRY COUPE
(serves 6)

This charming and lovely dessert is a combination of apricot ice and barely poached fresh black Bing cherries. The ice is made from a combination of canned apricots with a few dried ones added to intensify the flavor. The accompanying cherries are the World's Best Black Cherry Compote, from Chapter 2 of this book. The desserts are finished with small rosettes of whipped cream and topped with single black cherries. If you are artistic, try the alternate topping of a tiny apricot rose for a prettier finish to each dessert.

Although this dessert is fast, it should be started one or two days ahead to allow time for chilling and freezing.

INGREDIENTS:

4–6 ounces dried apricots

2 16-ounce cans apricots,
    packed in syrup

⅓ cup granulated sugar

1 cup whipping cream
    (total)

1½ tablespoons powdered
    sugar

1 recipe World's Best
    Black Cherry
    Compote

SERVING DISHES: 6 individual footed sherbet glasses or dessert saucers

SPECIAL EQUIPMENT NEEDED: An ice-cream scoop, 2¼ inches in diameter

PROCEDURE:

1. Set aside 12 dried apricots to be used for (optional) apricot roses for final decoration.

2. Place 12 dried apricots in a glass beaker. Add ¼ cup water, then cover and microwave 1 minute on high. Let sit 10 minutes.

3. Drain and discard syrup from 2 cans apricots, placing apricots into food processor fitted with steel blade. Add granulated sugar plus ¼ cup whipping cream. Add softened, dried apricots and process to a fairly smooth purée. Transfer to a bowl and freeze for 3 or 4 hours or overnight.

4. Cut frozen apricot mixture into pieces and process to a smooth, frozen slush, stopping machine occasionally to cut pieces further and to stir. Return to freezer and allow to chill again. Two or 3 hours before serving, check hardness of the ice and if necessary, return to processor and process until smooth again.

5. Whip balance of cream with powdered sugar and refrigerate until serving time.

TO SERVE: Remove cherries from syrup and drain on paper towels. Using an ice-cream scoop 2¼ inches in diameter, place a scoop of apricot ice in each dessert glass. Place a ring of drained cherries at the base of each mound of ice. Whip cream stiff again, then pipe a rosette on the top of each mound of ice. Top with either a black cherry or a dried apricot rose (see technique below).

DO-AHEAD INFORMATION: Cherry compote may be done several days ahead and kept in refrigerator. Apricot ice may be frozen a week or two ahead, but check consistency of ice several hours before serving as suggested above. Cream may be whipped 6 hours ahead or longer. Dried apricot roses may be done several days ahead and kept, covered with plastic, in refrigerator.

DRIED APRICOT ROSES: Place 4 dried apricot halves flat between sheets of waxed paper. Roll with rolling pin to flatten a bit. Place halves slightly overlapping, in a row, sticky sides up. Roll in a fairly tight roll, rolling in such a way as to roll 1 apricot half at a time, then meeting the next one and continuing to roll, and so on. Cut completed roll in half and place cut side down. Open up the petals, if necessary. Continue with other 8 apricot halves, 4 at a time, until you have 6 tiny roses.

BLUEBERRY COUPE
(serves 6)

This is a vanilla ice-cream coupe with blueberry ice plus a blueberry sauce containing whole blueberries. It is easy, delicious, and beautiful.

INGREDIENTS:

2 pints blueberries (total)   ¼–½ cup sugar
¾ cup apple juice   1 quart vanilla ice cream

SERVING DISHES: 6 stem glasses or individual dessert saucers

SPECIAL EQUIPMENT NEEDED: 2 ice-cream scoops, one 2¼ inches in diameter, the other 1½ inches

PROCEDURE:

1. Inspect blueberries, removing any stems or leaves. Set aside 1¼ cups berries to be used for sauce and garnish.

2. Place balance of blueberries in saucepan, adding apple juice plus ¼ cup sugar. Bring to a boil, stirring occasionally to help dissolve sugar, then simmer 1 minute. Dump into container of food processor fitted with steel blade. Process to a fairly smooth purée. Taste and decide whether to add more sugar or not. Remember, this is a dessert and it has to be somewhat sweet.

3. Measure out ¾ cup of the still hot blueberry purée and stir into reserved 1¼ cup blueberries. Taste this also. According to sweetness of berries, you may want to add a little more sugar. Refrigerate until serving time.

4. Place remaining blueberry purée in a bowl. Freeze 8 hours or overnight.

5. Three or 4 hours before serving, cut frozen blueberry purée into squares, then process in processor to a smooth slush. You may have to allow it 5 to 10 minutes to warm up a bit before it can be processed smoothly. Return to freezer to firm up a bit.

TO SERVE: Using 2¼-inch scoop, place a scoop of vanilla ice cream in each serving glass. Using a smaller scoop or a spoon, make an indentation in the top of the vanilla ice cream. Place a smaller scoop of blueberry ice in the depression so that it is partly inside and partly sticking out. Spoon berries in sauce at the base of the ice cream. Serve.

DO-AHEAD INFORMATION: Blueberry ice and blueberries in sauce may be prepared a day or 2 ahead. Coupes could be loaded with the vanilla ice cream, then frozen. Add blueberry ice and sauce just before serving.

COFFEE-CHOCOLATE COUPE
(serves 6)

This coupe is distinguished by a wonderful chocolate sauce made of cocoa, brown sugar, apple juice, and butter. The thin sauce, alive with unusual flavors, is served over scoops of coffee and chocolate ice cream. The coupes are decorated in a fanciful manner with whipped cream and chocolate coffee beans. Elegant and delicious.

INGREDIENTS:

¾ cup apple juice*

¾ cup (packed) dark
    brown sugar

⅓ cup cocoa (sifted)

2 tablespoons unsalted
    butter

1 teaspoon vanilla

1 cup whipping cream

1 tablespoon powdered
    sugar

1 quart coffee ice cream

1 pint chocolate ice cream

Chocolate mocha beans†

*If you prefer a thicker sauce, reduce apple juice by 2 tablespoons.
†These can be purchased, as either coffee-flavored chocolate molded in the shape of coffee beans or chocolate-coated espresso beans.

SERVING DISHES: 6 stem glasses or individual dessert saucers

SPECIAL EQUIPMENT NEEDED: 2 ice cream scoops, one 2¼ inches in diameter, the other 1½ inches

PROCEDURE:
1. Place apple juice, brown sugar, and cocoa in a saucepan. Bring to a boil, whisking to dissolve the cocoa. Cook 5 minutes, whisking occasionally, then transfer to a bowl. Add butter, cut into slices, and vanilla. Whisk until butter is melted. Refrigerate until chilled.

2. Whip cream with powdered sugar until stiff. Reserve in refrigerator until serving time.

3. Place a scoop of coffee ice cream in each serving glass. Using a smaller scoop, add a ball of chocolate ice cream on top. Wrap the glasses and the ice cream in plastic, then freeze until serving time.

TO SERVE: Spoon chocolate sauce around the bases of the coffee ice-cream scoops. Whisk cream stiff again; then, using a small open star tip (#3 or #4), pipe 4 or 5 lines of whipped cream on each dessert, going from the base of the large coffee ball to the top of the small chocolate ball. Pipe a small rosette on the very top. Place a mocha bean in each rosette. Serve.

DO-AHEAD INFORMATION: Coupes may be loaded and frozen a week or more ahead, but if they freeze rock-hard, you may want to bring them out to the room 20 to 30 minutes before serving. The chocolate sauce may be made several days ahead and kept in the refrigerator. Cream may be whipped 6 to 8 hours ahead and kept, covered with plastic, in refrigerator.

TOASTED HAZELNUT COUPE
(serves 6)

The flavor of toasted hazelnuts is one of the great European ice-cream and candy flavors and yet it is still relatively unknown here in the United States. If you are not familiar with it, you have a wonderful treat in store.

In this coupe, toasted hazelnuts (also known as filberts) are chopped and stirred into vanilla ice cream. A scoop of the resulting hazelnut ice cream is served on a larger scoop of vanilla ice cream, then a chocolate sauce is dribbled over and around and more chopped, toasted hazelnuts are sprinkled over all.

INGREDIENTS:

4 ounces unsweetened
    chocolate
2 tablespoons unsalted
    butter
½ cup sugar

1 cup apple juice
8 ounces hazelnuts (or
    filberts)*
1 quart vanilla ice cream

SERVING DISHES: 6 stem glasses or individual dessert saucers

SPECIAL EQUIPMENT NEEDED: 2 ice cream scoops, one 2¼ inches in diameter, the other 1½ inches
*Whole blanched almonds could be used instead.

PROCEDURE:

1. Preheat oven to 350 degrees.

2. Place chocolate, butter, sugar, and ½ cup apple juice in a saucepan. Heat, stirring with a wire whisk, until it comes to a boil and is smooth. Add balance of apple juice, then return to a boil and allow to cook for 5 minutes, whisking occasionally. Transfer to a bowl, then refrigerate until chilled.

3. Place hazelnuts in a single layer on a baking sheet. Bake in preheated 350 degree oven 15 to 20 minutes, or until lightly toasted. Let cool a bit, then rub off only the loose skins that come off. Do not waste time trying to skin these, as the skin is good for you and you'll never know it's in there.

4. Chop nuts into ¼-inch dice, either by using a heavy knife or by pulsing in the food processor.

5. Place ¼ of the vanilla ice cream (8 ounces, or 1 cup packed down) into a bowl. Add ⅔ of the chopped toasted hazelnuts. Mix into the ice cream, then return to freezer and freeze until firm, 6 to 8 hours, or overnight. Reserve balance of chopped nuts in plastic.

6. Place a large scoop of vanilla ice cream into each of 6 serving glasses. Place smaller scoops (1 to 2 tablespoon capacity) of hazelnut ice cream on top. Wrap glasses and ice cream in plastic and reserve in freezer until serving time.

TO SERVE: Stir chocolate sauce. Dribble a few thin streaks over each coupe, then spoon more around the base of the vanilla ice cream. Sprinkle with chopped nuts. Serve.

DO-AHEAD INFORMATION: Nuts may be chopped and sauce prepared 3 or 4 days ahead, or longer, and stored in refrigerator. Glasses may be packed with ice cream and stored, wrapped in plastic, in freezer several days ahead. Remove from refrigerator 20 to 30 minutes before serving so that the ice cream is not rock-hard.

LEMON COUPE WITH CANDIED PEEL
(serves 6)

This lovely yellow-and-white coupe is a real delight for lemon lovers. It consists of vanilla ice cream topped with a deep yellow, sweet-tart lemon sauce (also known as lemon curd), decorated with candied lemon peel. It is a perfect dessert for a luncheon or light dinner.

For this coupe, you would normally prepare just the sauce and the peel; however, good-quality lemon curd is available in bottles in specialty food shops. If you can find it in your area, all you will need to prepare is the candied peel.

INGREDIENTS:

5 medium-large lemons (total)

1½ cups sugar (total)

1 stick (4 ounces) unsalted butter

6 egg yolks

1 quart vanilla ice cream

SERVING DISHES: 6 stem glasses or individual dessert saucers

SPECIAL EQUIPMENT NEEDED: 1 ice-cream scoop, 2¼ inches in diameter

PROCEDURE:

1. Bring 3 cups of water to boil in a saucepan. Using a lemon zester (a hand tool with 5 small holes at one end), scrape down 3 lemons to get long shreds of peel. Place peel in boiling water and simmer for 5 minutes, or until tender. Drain, rinse once or twice, then drain again.

2. Bring ½ cup sugar plus ½ cup water to a boil in a small saucepan, stirring occasionally to dissolve the sugar. Place drained peel in the hot syrup; remove from heat and allow to cool. Store peel in syrup in refrigerator.

3. Grate zest from 2 remaining lemons and place in a heavy saucepan (can be of any material except uncoated aluminum). Squeeze lemons (do not strain); should make 1 cup of juice. Add lemon juice, 1 cup sugar, and yolks. Whisk to mix. Add butter, cut into slices. Place over medium-high heat for 2 minutes, or until very warm to the touch. Lower heat to medium-low; then, whisking constantly, heat for another 4 or 5 minutes or until you see the *first signs* of boiling. Stop whisking now and then to look for the signs. Dump the hot lemon sauce into a clean bowl and whisk briefly until smooth. Refrigerate, uncovered, until chilled. Cover and reserve in refrigerator.

TO SERVE: At serving time, place 1 scoop of vanilla ice cream in each stem glass. Whisk sauce until smooth, then spoon 3 or 4 tablespoonsful over each. If using bottled lemon curd and it is too thick, thin with water or lemon juice. Remove lemon peel from syrup with a fork, placing small mounds over desserts. Serve.

DO-AHEAD INFORMATION: Both the lemon peel and curd keep in the refrigerator for weeks.

MAPLE PECAN COUPE
(serves 6)

This dessert is a miracle; it is so simple and so good. It consists of vanilla ice cream with slightly thickened maple syrup, topped with toasted pecans. It is probably the easiest dessert in the book and for me, it is one of the best-tasting.

INGREDIENTS:

1½ cups (4–5 ounces) pecans

1 cup (8 ounces) maple syrup
1 quart vanilla ice cream*

SERVING DISHES: 6 stem glasses or individual dessert saucers

SPECIAL EQUIPMENT NEEDED: 1 ice-cream scoop, 2¼ inches in diameter

PROCEDURE:

1. Spread pecans on baking sheet and bake in preheated 350-degree oven 12 to 13 minutes, or until lightly toasted. If pecans are small, they can be left whole. If large, chop into ½-inch dice. Reserve.

2. Place maple syrup in freezer and allow to remain 3 hours or longer, or overnight. The syrup will thicken slightly.

TO SERVE: Place scoops of vanilla ice cream in serving glasses. Spoon 1 or 2 tablespoons of maple syrup over each dessert, then sprinkle with toasted pecans. Serve.

*You could substitute a good-quality maple pecan ice cream.

DO-AHEAD INFORMATION: Everything can be prepared and frozen 1 or 2 weeks before serving.

PEARS IN SPICED RED WINE COUPE
(serves 6)

This coupe is based on the well-known French dessert, Pears in Spiced Red Wine. The pears become an ice (or sorbet, to be a little fancier) that is served with diced pears in a syrup flavored with pear or orange liqueur. The coupes are topped with whipped cream and candied violets to accentuate the wonderful color of the ice.

INGREDIENTS:

1½ cups red wine*
⅓ cup granulated sugar
¹⁄₁₆ teaspoon nutmeg
3 very thin slices lemon peel (removed with vegetable peeler)
2 whole cloves
½ teaspoon cinnamon

2 29-ounce cans pears in syrup (total)
1–2 tablespoons pear (or orange) liqueur
1 cup whipping cream (total)
2 tablespoons powdered sugar
6 candied violets†

SERVING DISHES: 6 stem glasses or serving saucers

SPECIAL EQUIPMENT NEEDED: 1 ice-cream scoop, 2¼ inches in diameter

*An inexpensive mountain red or "hearty" Burgundy works fine for this.
†Candied violets are available in specialty food shops.

PROCEDURE:

1. To make the ice, put first 6 ingredients in a saucepan and bring to a boil. Simmer 5 minutes, then reserve.

2. Open 1 can of pears and drain, discarding syrup. Slice pears and place in food processor fitted with steel blade. Fish lemon peel out of wine mixture and add to pears in processor. Process to a smooth purée.

3. Remove whole cloves from wine mixture and discard. Add mixture to pear purée in processor and process 1 or 2 seconds to mix. Transfer to bowl, then place in freezer and freeze until hard, several hours or overnight.

4. For the diced-pear accompaniment, measure out ¾ cup of syrup from remaining can of pears. Place in a bowl and add pear or orange liqueur to taste. Cut the pears into ½-inch dice, then place in syrup. Cover and reserve in refrigerator until serving time.

5. Three hours before serving, chop frozen pear-wine mixture and place in food processor fitted with steel blade. Add 2 tablespoons whipping cream and process until smooth. You may have to let this sit in the room 10 minutes to warm up before it will process well. Return to freezer. Check 15 minutes before serving and, if necessary, remove from freezer to soften a bit.

6. Whip balance of cream with powdered sugar and reserve in refrigerator until serving time.

TO SERVE: Place a scoop of pears-in-red-wine ice in each serving glass. Spoon diced pears in syrup on the side. Whisk whipped cream stiff again, then pipe a rosette on top of each mound of ice. Top with a candied violet. Serve.

DO-AHEAD INFORMATION: The ice may be prepared and frozen a week ahead or more. Diced pears in sauce and whipped cream may be prepared 6 to 8 hours before serving. Process ice 3 hours before serving.

PECAN BALLS WITH BROWN SUGAR SAUCE
(serves 6)

If you have ever been to Pittsburgh, you have probably eaten Pecan Balls. This dessert is so popular and so readily available in restaurants there that many Pittsburgh people are astonished to learn it is not known nationally.

Pecan Balls are very simple to make and they are really good. For each serving, a scoop of vanilla ice cream is rolled in pecans, then served with either a brown sugar sauce or a chocolate sauce, depending upon your preference. I prefer the brown sugar sauce, especially the one described below, but if you prefer chocolate, try the thick chocolate sauce from the Toasted Hazelnut Coupe.

INGREDIENTS:

1 cup (packed) dark
    brown sugar
½ stick (2 ounces)
    unsalted butter
⅓ cup apple juice

1 teaspoon vanilla
1 quart vanilla ice cream
8 ounces (approximately)
    pecans

SERVING DISHES: 6 individual dessert saucers or glasses

SPECIAL EQUIPMENT NEEDED: An ice-cream scoop, 2¼ inches in diameter

PROCEDURE:

1. Place brown sugar, butter cut into thin slices, and apple juice in a small saucepan. Bring to a boil, stirring to dissolve the sugar and melt the butter. Cook at a medium boil for 5 minutes. Remove from heat and add vanilla. Transfer to a bowl and chill in refrigerator. Whisk or stir once or twice as it cools; then, when completely chilled, beat with an electric mixer until pale and smooth. Add an extra tablespoon of apple juice if it is too thick.

2. Scoop out 6 portions of vanilla ice cream, giving the balls one flat surface so they can sit on the saucers. Roll or stud the ice cream in whole, small pecans, or in coarse chopped pecans. The balls should be almost completely covered with the pecans. Place on chilled individual dessert saucers, then wrap each in plastic and return to freezer.

TO SERVE: Check hardness of ice cream and, if necessary, remove desserts from freezer 20 minutes before serving so that ice cream is not rock-hard. Stir sauce, then spoon 2-tablespoon portions around the base of each pecan ball. Serve.

DO-AHEAD INFORMATION: Sauce may be prepared a week or more ahead and kept in refrigerator. Pecan Balls may be assembled and kept in freezer a week ahead or longer.

RASPBERRY COUPE WITH GRAND MARNIER
(serves 6)

Here is another of those miraculous desserts that takes 10 minutes to do, yet tastes like a million dollars. The recipe calls for frozen raspberries (and the dish is wonderful with them); however, if fresh raspberries are available, by all means use them. Check fresh berries for sweetness and, if desired, add a tablespoon or two of sugar when adding the Grand Marnier.

INGREDIENTS:

3 10-ounce packages
     frozen raspberries,
     packed with sugar
     (defrosted)
3 tablespoons Grand
     Marnier*

1 cup whipping cream
2 tablespoons powdered
     sugar
1 quart vanilla ice cream

SERVING DISHES: 6 individual stem glasses

SPECIAL EQUIPMENT NEEDED: An ice cream scoop, 2¼ inches in diameter

PROCEDURE:

1. Drain raspberries, reserving juice for another use. Choose 6 of the largest, prettiest berries and set aside in refrigerator for final decoration. Place balance of berries in a bowl. Add Grand Marnier and stir carefully. Cover and reserve in refrigerator.

2. Whip cream with powdered sugar. Cover and reserve in refrigerator.

3. Fill serving glasses approximately ⅔ full with vanilla ice cream. Cover with plastic, then reserve in freezer.

TO SERVE: Spoon raspberries with liqueur over ice cream

*Cointreau is equally good; orange curaçao will do.

and spoon or pipe whipped cream on top. Place one of the reserved raspberries on top of each dessert. Serve.

DO-AHEAD INFORMATION: Ice cream may be placed in glasses several days ahead and kept in freezer, but check for hardness several hours ahead, and if ice cream is rock-hard, remove glasses from freezer ½ hour before serving. Raspberries may be prepared and cream may be whipped 6 to 8 hours ahead. Reserve both in refrigerator. At serving time, whip cream stiff again if necessary.

FROZEN CHOCOLATE SQUARES
(serves 6 to 9)

These beautiful chocolate squares consist of a chocolate cake base, a chocolate ice-cream filling, and a chocolate coating. They are decorated with a large rosette of whipped cream, then topped with Godiva chocolate "daisy" medallions. The resulting frozen squares are fast, fabulous, and truly gorgeous.

This recipe looks long and complicated, but it isn't. The cake uses a super-easy one-saucepan method. The entire dessert probably requires no more than 30 minutes of actual work to be done, but as time is required for baking, cooling, spreading ice cream, and refreezing, you will need to start at least a day ahead.

INGREDIENTS:

½ cup all-purpose flour
½ teaspoon baking *soda*
1 ounce unsweetened
  chocolate
5½ tablespoons unsalted
  butter (total)
½ cup granulated sugar
¼ cup milk
1 egg

1 quart chocolate ice
  cream*
4 ounces semisweet
  chocolate
1 tablespoon light corn
  syrup
1 cup whipping cream
2 tablespoons powdered
  sugar
6 chocolate medallions†

COOKING UTENSIL AND SERVING DISHES: An 8-inch square baking tin or ovenproof dish, and 6–9 serving saucers or plates

PROCEDURE:

1. Preheat oven to 350 degrees. Place a folded strip of aluminum foil, approximately 20 inches long, across the tin so that it goes down one side, across the bottom, and up the other side, allowing flaps to hang out both sides. Tuck the flaps under the tin. You will use these flaps later to help remove the finished dessert.

2. Sift flour to measure, then stir in baking soda. Place mixture in sifter and reserve.

3. Place unsweetened chocolate with 1½ tablespoons of butter into a 1½-quart saucepan. Heat carefully, stirring and breaking up the butter and chocolate, until mixture is melted and smooth.

*Try to find a good-quality dark chocolate ice cream. If you like chocolate, but not all that much, try vanilla or coffee ice cream in this instead.
†I used 6 dark, all-chocolate Godiva daisy medallions. Any fairly flat, pretty, European-type chocolate will do, either dark or light.

4. Add granulated sugar and milk. Stir until sugar is dissolved, heating slightly, if necessary, until mixture is barely warm. Add the egg and whisk to break it up. Sift in flour and soda, then stir with a wire whisk until flour is completely mixed in, but do not overwork. Dump batter into baking tin. Tilt to get batter (there isn't very much) into corners.

5. Bake in preheated 350-degree oven 17 to 20 minutes, or until it feels done to the touch. Don't peek before 15 minutes. Chocolate cakes are delicate and fall easily. Cool on rack in tin, then freeze in tin.

6. Let ice cream soften a bit, if rock-hard. Spread in an even layer over frozen cake. If necessary, do not use all the ice cream. It is important that ice-cream level be below the sides of tin to keep chocolate coating in later. The ice-cream layer must be very level. I cover it with plastic, then take a box (a tea box the last time) and rub it over the ice cream to level it. Freeze for several hours.

7. For the chocolate coating, place semisweet chocolate, light corn syrup, and 4 tablespoons of butter in a glass beaker. Cover with plastic, then microwave on high for 1 minute. Stir and cut up butter and chocolate lumps, then microwave another 30 seconds, or until quite warm but not too hot.

8. It is important that the coating be poured while it is still warm. You must work quickly, as it starts to set right away and it melts the ice cream a little. Remove plastic from ice cream. Have a rubber spatula on the side. Dump out all the coating in center of ice cream, frantically scraping out the last part from beaker. Right away, tilt baking tin left and right, then front and back, to get chocolate in a fairly even coating. Stop. Set tin down on counter. Don't worry about being perfect as most of this is to be covered with whipped

cream and a medallion, but be happy to get it just fairly even. Let baking tin sit without touching it for 1 or 2 minutes, or until coating is set. Cover with plastic and return to freezer.

9. Whip cream with powdered sugar. Refrigerate.

TO SERVE: Cut down sides of baking tin where there is no foil to free cake and ice cream. Lift out cake, using foil flaps. Cut cake into 9 squares. Place on serving saucers. Whip cream again until stiff, then pipe a large rosette on top of each square. Place chocolate medallions on top. Give everyone a knife and a fork for eating these.

DO-AHEAD INFORMATION: Cake, ice cream, and chocolate coating may be prepared a week ahead or longer and kept in freezer. Cream may be whipped 8 hours ahead. Check squares ½ hour before serving and if too hard, remove from freezer to soften a little. Add piped cream and medallions just before serving.

CHOCOLATE TOASTED-ALMOND ICE-CREAM BOMBE
(serves 6 to 8)

Ice-cream molds are fun and festive. This bombe-shaped or round mold is lined with chocolate ice cream, then filled with toasted-almond ice cream. The bombe is unmolded and decorated with whipped-cream rosettes, red sour cherries, and toasted chopped almonds. It is an elegant, glamorous dessert.

As with all frozen desserts, start this one at least a day ahead to allow time for it to freeze firm.

INGREDIENTS:

8 ounces blanched almonds

1 quart chocolate ice cream

1 pint vanilla ice cream

1 cup whipping cream

2 tablespoons powdered sugar

1 21-ounce can cherry pie filling

1–2 tablespoons kirsch or orange liqueur (optional)

SERVING DISH: A round china serving platter

ICE-CREAM MOLD: A 4- to 5-cup-capacity bowl with as round a shape as possible

PROCEDURE:

1. Preheat oven to 350 degrees.

2. Place a folded-over band of foil about 3 inches wide into the mold in such a way that it goes across the bottom and up the sides and allows 3- or 4-inch-long flaps to extend out each side. Chill bowl in freezer 5 minutes.

3. Spread almonds 1 layer deep on a baking sheet. Bake in preheated 350-degree oven 15 to 20 minutes (stirring once halfway through) or until golden brown. Cool.

4. Cut or spoon ¾-inch-thick slices of chocolate ice cream and line the bowl with them. Cut and piece. When the sides are covered, line hole with plastic and, using your fist or a large spoon, pack the ice cream to make as smooth a lining as possible. Freeze for 1 hour.

5. Chop toasted almonds into ¼-inch dice using a large knife or pulsing in the food processor. Reserve ¼ chopped

almonds for decoration later. Place balance into a bowl, adding the vanilla ice cream. Poke and stir until nuts are incorporated into the ice cream.

6. Remove plastic from chocolate-ice-cream-lined bowl. Smooth ice-cream lining, then dump in almond ice-cream mixture. Level top, then return to freezer to freeze hard.

7. Whip cream with powdered sugar until stiff. Reserve in refrigerator.

8. Place contents of can of cherries in a sieve, over a bowl. Bang to eliminate red starchy filling. Place cherries in a bowl. Stir in optional kirsch or orange liqueur. Reserve in refrigerator.

9. Place serving dish in freezer to chill for 5 minutes. Dip bottom of ice-cream mold in cold water for 10 seconds. Invert, pulling gently on the foil flaps. Unmold bombe onto chilled serving dish. Remove foil and smooth surface of bombe with a knife. Cover with plastic and return to freezer.

10. Drain cherries on a towel. Whip cream again until stiff. Decorate bombe by piping fairly large (#5 or #6 open star tip) flattened rosettes of cream over the surface. You can let some of the chocolate show through. Place a red cherry in each rosette. Sprinkle reserved chopped almonds on top and toss some on sides. Freeze uncovered until cream has set then wrap in plastic.

TO SERVE: Remove bombe from freezer 30 minutes before serving so cherries have a chance to soften a bit. Serve in wedges. You could serve chocolate sauce on the side.

DO-AHEAD INFORMATION: The mold can be packed with the ice creams a week or more ahead and kept in the freezer.

Whipped-cream rosettes and red cherries may be added 5 or 6 hours before serving.

FLEUR-DE-LYS
(serves 6)

I am thrilled with how beautiful, how elegant, and yet how easy this dessert is to do. It is the epitome of fast and fabulous. If you try nothing else in this whole book, I hope you will make this one.

The dessert consists of pyramids of 4 small scoops of different ice creams and ices, served on flat dessert plates. The scoops on the plates are outlined with scrolls and rosettes of whipped cream flavored with Grand Marnier. Coarsely chopped macadamia nuts are sprinkled over all. The colors, shapes, scrolls, and rosettes are so lovely that the plates look like emblems or fleurs-de-lys. It is one of the prettiest desserts I have ever seen.

INGREDIENTS:

1 pint each of four different sorbets, sherbets, ices, *gelati,* or ice creams

1 cup whipping cream

2 tablespoons powdered sugar

1 tablespoon Grand Marnier

3½ ounces macadamia nuts

SERVING DISHES: 6 attractive dessert plates, approximately 8 inches in diameter (I have 6 blue-and-white Spode dessert plates that are beautiful for this dessert)

SPECIAL EQUIPMENT NEEDED: A small ice cream scoop, 1½ inches in diameter

PROCEDURE:

1. Place serving dishes in the freezer for 10 minutes or until well chilled. Scoop out ice creams and ices, placing three different-flavored balls in a triangle in the center of each plate, and placing a fourth ice-cream ball on the top, using your prettiest color. The last time I did this, I used chocolate and coffee ice cream and lemon ice for the bottom 3, and strawberry ice on the top.

2. Wrap plates and ice cream with plastic, then reserve in freezer until serving time. If you do this several days ahead, check hardness of ice creams 20 minutes before serving, and if ice creams are rock-hard, remove from freezer to soften a bit.

3. Whip cream with powdered sugar until stiff. Stir in Grand Marnier. Reserve in refrigerator until serving time.

4. Check macadamia nuts and if they are too salty, rub with a towel. Chop nuts into ¼-inch dice. Reserve.

TO SERVE: Whip cream stiff again; then, using a pastry bag with a #5 or #6 open-star tip, pipe whipped cream on the plates as if to outline the 3 balls of ice cream. Place small rosettes of cream at the 3 places where the balls meet. Sprinkle macadamia nuts over the dessert to look good. Serve.

DO-AHEAD INFORMATION: Plates with ice cream may be prepared a day or more ahead. Cream may be whipped and nuts may be chopped 6 to 8 hours ahead or longer.

STRAWBERRY-BANANA ICE-CREAM RING
(serves 8 to 10)

This is a lovely and delicious dessert for an important occasion. It consists of a ring of strawberry and vanilla ice cream decorated with apricot-glazed bananas, piped whipped cream, and whole fresh strawberries. The strawberry ice cream (in this case, a commercial one) gets a flavor boost from the fresh strawberry purée that is added to it, while more of the same purée, with sliced strawberries added, becomes a sauce to accompany the dessert.

INGREDIENTS:

3 pints strawberries
5 tablespoons granulated
   sugar (total)
1 pint strawberry ice
   cream
¾ quart vanilla ice cream

1 cup whipping cream
2 tablespoons powdered
   sugar
1 8-ounce jar apricot jam
3–4 bananas

SERVING DISH: An attractive, round, china platter

RING MOLD: A 1½-quart ring mold, or a 12-cup mold (a bundt tin, for example) filled only half full

PROCEDURE:

  1. Look through strawberries, setting aside 8 attractive ones for final decoration. Brush, hull, and refrigerate. If strawberries need washing, do it 1 or 2 hours before serving.*

  2. Brush (or wash, if necessary, and dry well) and hull

*If strawberries are washed and stored somewhat wet, they can rot overnight, even in the refrigerator.

the balance of the berries, then place ⅔ of them in container of food processor fitted with steel blade. Add 4 tablespoons granulated sugar, then process to a purée. Taste and add more sugar if desired. Refrigerate. Slice the balance of the strawberries and place in a bowl. Sprinkle over remaining 1 tablespoon sugar, then stir, cover, and refrigerate.

3. Place a band of plastic or foil across the mold, letting it run down into the mold, up in the center, then down on the other side. Allow 2 flaps to stick out. Place strawberry ice cream in a mixing bowl. Add 1 cup strawberry purée. Stir and poke until well mixed, then dump into mold. Pack down to avoid air holes. You may take time to let this firm in the freezer for 3 or 4 hours, or go ahead and add slightly softened vanilla ice cream right away. (It won't matter if the 2 layers get mixed up a little.) Cover with plastic. Level as best you can, then freeze 6 to 8 hours or overnight.

4. Whip cream with powdered sugar until stiff, then reserve in refrigerator.

5. Place apricot jam in food processor and process until fairly smooth. Return to jar and reserve in refrigerator.

6. Place serving dish in freezer to chill.

TO SERVE: At serving time, warm some of the apricot jam in a small saucepan. Thin with 1 tablespoon water. Unmold ring onto chilled serving dish by dipping mold bottom in cold water and pulling carefully on plastic or foil flaps. Peel bananas, cut into 2-inch sections (or as high as the ice-cream ring), then cut each section in half lengthwise. Make sure bottoms are level so that they will stand up with no trouble. Stand 8 to 10 banana pairs up in the style of open books all around the ring. Brush these with apricot jam. Whisk cream to get it stiff again; then, using a pastry bag fitted with a large open-star tip, pipe *flammes* of whipped cream in the spaces where the banana pairs are split. Pipe 8 large rosettes on the top of the ring, then place reserved 8 whole strawberries in the rosettes. Stir sugared berries into remaining strawberry purée, then pass this sauce around at the table.

DO-AHEAD INFORMATION: Strawberries may be puréed and sliced a day ahead and ice-cream mold done at the same time. Jam may be processed weeks ahead. Cream may be whipped 6 to 8 hours ahead.

INDEX

Almond(s)
  Chocolate Toasted-, Ice-Cream
    Bombe, 274
  Cream Pie, 116
  Crust, for Almond Cream Pie, 116
  to glaze, 30, 66
    See also Glazing techniques
  Ground, Cake, 149
  Light Carrot, Cake, 158
  Mocha Torte, 202
  Shortbread Crust, for Strawberry
    Pie, 133
Amaretto, flavoring whipped cream,
  14
Ambrosia (Sour Cream Fruit) Pie, 131
Angel Food, Pineapple, Trifle, 196
Apple(s)
  Baked
    with Marbleized Cranberry
      Sauce, 52
    with Walnut Brown Sugar
      Sauce, 53
  Chunky Spiced, Cake, 150
  Crisp, 55
    apples for, 55
  Pecan Cake, 152
  Spiced, Brownie Trifle, 180
  Spiced Custard with, 77
Applesauce, Raspberry-, Cake-Tart,
  235
Apricot(s)
  –Bing Cherry Coupe, 255
  Cake-Tart, 232
  dried roses (decoration), 257
  -Pineapple Cheesecake, 138
  (in) Sour Cream Fruit Pie, 131

Baba, Chocolate, Cake, 159
Baked Apples
  with Marbleized Cranberry Sauce,
    52
  with Walnut Brown Sugar Sauce,
    53
Baking pans
  buttering and flouring, 15–16
  cast-iron skillet as, 171
  glass vs. tin, 148
  lining with parchment, 15
  for pies, 115
  springform, 16
Baking techniques
  for cakes, 15–22, 148
  for custards, 76–77
  for pies, 115–116
  for spongecakes, 15–22
Banana(s)
  Blueberries and, with English
    Cream, 26
  Chips, Chocolate English Cream
    with, 95
  Cream Pie, Macaroon Crust, 118
  Macaroon English Cream, 92
  (in) Sour Cream Fruit Pie, 131
  Spiced Pecan Torte with, 216
  Strawberry-, Ice-Cream Ring,
    279
Basic Butter Spongecake Layers,
  228
  baking hints, 15–22
  mixing bowls, 17
  splitting layers, 21–22
  as spongecake base, 225–26, 240,
    242, 245

unmolding, 20–21
See also Spongecakes
Bavarian Cream Trifle with
    Strawberries, 186
Berries, to flour, 154
Blackberry
    Kuchen, 153
    Sauce, Sliced Peaches in, 32
Blueberry(ies)
    and Bananas with English Cream,
        26
    Compote with Glazed Nut
        Topping, 58
    Coupe, 257
    Custard, 83
        in kuchen, substituting for
            other fruit, 154
    (in) Mixed Fruit in Cantaloupe
        Rings, 31
    Mountain Cake, 204
    Peaches with, in Raspberry
        Cream, 34
    poaching, 51
    Trifle, 182
Bombe, Chocolate Toasted-Almond
        Ice-Cream, 274
Bread Pudding
    Old-Fashioned, 80
    Raisin, with Peanut Butter, 81
Brown Sugar
    English Cream with Glazed
        Pecans, 93
    Icing, Cream Cheese, for Brown
        Sugar Pecan Squares, 157
    Pecan Squares, 155
    Pineapple with Coconut, and
        Rum, 41
    Sauce
        Pecan Balls with, 268
        Walnut, Baked Apples with, 53
Brownie(s)
    Butterscotch Pecan (Brown Sugar
        Pecan Squares), 155
    Spiced Apple, Trifle, 180
Bundt Cake, Chocolate Syrup, with
        Grand Marnier, 165

Butter(s)
    almond, 65
    gianduja, 65
    hazelnut, 65
    vs. margarine, 8–9
    ratio of, in cake, 19
    Spongecake
        Chocolate, 230
        Layers, Basic, 228
        Tart Shell, 226
        See also Cake-Tarts; Spongecakes,
            Baking techniques
Butterscotch, Grapes in Rum,
        Cream, 28

Cake(s)
    Apple Pecan, 152
    Baking techniques, 15–22, 148
        beating eggs, 10–11, 17–18
        cutting into layers, 21–22
        freezing layers, 22
        measuring flour, 16–17
        mixing bowls, size of, 17
        mixing ingredients, 148
        oven peeking, 19–20
        positioning two cakes, 16
        refrigerating layers, 22
        for spongecakes, 15–22
        steps in, 18
        testing for doneness, 18–20
        toothpick test, 19
        unmolding, 20–21
        warming ingredients, 148
    Blackberry Kuchen, 153
    Blueberry Mountain, 204
    Brown Sugar Pecan Squares, 155
    butter in, 19
    Caramel Pecan Surprise, 240
    Cherry Dome, 207
    Chocolate
        Baba, 159
        -Coated Pear, 242
        Cream, 209
        Mousse
            Loaf, 214
            with Strawberries, 212

Sauce, 164
Syrup Bundt, with Grand
 Marnier, 165
Chunky Spiced Apple, 150
Filled Poppy-Seed, 173
Ground Almond, 149
Light Carrot Almond, 158
Lime Meringue, 245
Nana's Gingerbread, 168
Orange Liqueur, with Walnuts
 and Raisins, 169
pans, 148
 buttering and flouring, 15–16
 lining with parchment, 15
 springform, 16
Pineapple Pecan Upside-Down, 171
Queen of Sheba Chocolate
 Squares, 162
racks, unmolding onto, 20–21
Strawberry Taj Mahal, 247
types of, to use in trifles, 179
See also Cake-Tarts; Cheesecakes;
 Spongecakes; Tortes
Cake-Tart(s)
Apricot, 232
invention of, 225
Pineapple-Coconut, 233
Raspberry-Applesauce, 235
Shell, Butter Spongecake, 226
Tangerine, 238
Candied peel
Lemon Coupe with, 263
Lime Mousse with, 101
to prepare, 101–102
Candied violets, 266
Cantaloupe, Mixed Fruit in, Rings, 31
Caramel Pecan Surprise Cake, 240
Carrot
(flavored) cream, 159
Light, Almond Cake, 158
-Lime Cream, Pineapple with, 39
Cast-iron skillet, baking
 upside-down cake in, 171
Chantilly
Creme, 42
Purple Plums, 42

Charlotte Portugaise, 190
Cheesecake
Apricot-Pineapple, 138
No-Bake Lemon, 140
Raspberry, 142
Cherry(ies)
Apricot–Bing, Coupe, 255
Black, Custard, 78
Dome Cake, 207
poaching, 51, 56
World's Best Black, Compote,
 56
Chocolate
Baba Cake, 159
Butter Spongecake, 230
-Coated Pear Cake, 242
Coffee-, Coupe, 259
Cream Cake, 209
curls, preparing, 29
English Cream with Banana
 Chips, 95
Frozen, Squares, 271
grid, 242
icing, creating a spiderweb effect,
 211
melting in double boiler, 13
Mousse
 Cake with Strawberries, 212
 Loaf, 214
 Marquise Surprise, 97
Pear Betty, 63
Pie, Walnut Chocolate Crust, 120
Queen of Sheba, Squares, 162
Sauce
 Cake, 164
 cocoa–brown sugar–apple
  juice–butter, with a coupe,
  259
 Pear Surprise with, 65
 Strawberries with Chocolate
  Cream and, 44
sheets, 248–49
Syrup Bundt Cake with Grand
 Marnier, 165
Toasted-Almond Ice-Cream
 Bombe, 274

Truffle(s)
  made from extra chocolate
    coating, 244
  Trifle, 184
  Walnut, Crust, for Chocolate Pie,
    120
Chunky Spiced Apple Cake, 150
Citrus fruit
  peel, candied, 101–102
  zest of, 11–12
Clafouti, variation on, 78
Coconut
  Crust, for Sour Cream Fruit Pie, 131
  Custard Pie, Magic Deep-Dish, 122
  Pineapple with, Brown Sugar, and
    Rum, 41
  Pineapple-, Cake-Tart, 233
Coffee
  (in) Almond Mocha Torte, 202
  -Chocolate Coupe, 259
Cointreau
  Cream, Strawberries and Kiwis in,
    Frozen, 45
  flavoring whipped cream, 14, 56
  See also Liqueurs
Compote
  Blueberry, with Glazed Nut
    Topping, 58
  Rhubarb, with Fresh Strawberries,
    70
  World's Best Black Cherry, 56
Cookies
  as pie crust, 113–14
    almond, 116
    coconut macaroon, 118
    lemon nut, 138, 140
    molasses, 129, 142
    shortbread, 133
  as tart base, for Mini Strawberry
    Tarts, 136
Coupe
  Apricot–Bing Cherry, 255
  Blueberry, 257
  Coffee-Chocolate, 259
  Lemon, with Candied Peel, 263
  Maple Pecan, 265

Pears in Spiced Red Wine, 266
Pecan Balls with Brown Sugar
  Sauce, 268
Raspberry, with Grand Marnier,
  269
Toasted Hazelnut, 261
Cranberry
  Custard, 84
  Sauce
    Marbleized, Baked Apples with,
    52
    -Orange, Pears with, 37
Cream
  carrot, 159
  Carrot-Lime, Pineapple with, 39
  Chocolate, Strawberries with, and
    Chocolate Sauce, 44
  Cointreau, Strawberries and Kiwis
    in, Frozen, 45
  Lemon, with White Raisins in
    Grand Marnier, 99
  Pecan Praline, 103
  Raspberry, Peaches with
    Blueberries in, 34
  Rum Butterscotch, Grapes in, 28
  Sherried, 29
  Walnut Torte with Peaches and,
    219
  See also English Cream; Sour
    Cream; Whipped Cream
Cream Cheese Brown Sugar Icing,
  157
Crème Anglaise, 179
Creme Chantilly, 42
Crisp
  Crisp Apple, 55
  Plum, 68
Crust
  Almond
    for Almond Cream Pie, 116
    Shortbread, for Strawberry Pie,
    133
  Chopped Peanut, for Peanut
    Butter Cream Pie, 128
  Coconut, for Sour Cream Fruit
    Pie, 131

Macaroon, for Banana Cream Pie,
    118
Molasses
    Pecan, for No-Bake Pumpkin
        Pie, 129
    for Raspberry Cheesecake, 142
    Walnut Chocolate, for Chocolate
        Pie, 120
Custard(s)
    baking techniques
        cooking in water bath, 76
        hints, 76–77
        testing for doneness, 76–77
        wiggle test, 76–77
    Black Cherry, 78
    freezing, 77
    fruit-based, 75
        Blueberry, 83
        Cranberry, 84
        Orange, 85
        Strawberry-Raspberry, 87
    Pie, Magic Deep-Dish Coconut,
        122
    refrigerating, 77
    Spiced, with Apples, 77

Decorating techniques
    chocolate
        grid, 242
        sheet, 248–49
    for coupe, 260
    dried apricot roses, 257
    flammes, 237, 280
    piping with whipped cream, 14–15
        on cookie tart, 136–37
        on pies, 114–15
    spiderweb effect, with chocolate
        icing, 211
Deep-Dish Pie, Magic, Coconut
    Custard, 122

Eccles cakes, variation of, 135
Egg(s)
    warming, 148
    whites

beating with electric mixer, 11,
    17–18
inverted bowl test, 11
overbeating, problems of, 10–11
yolks
    beating, 10
        with electric mixer, 17
        for spongecakes, 10
    effect of sugar on, 148
Electric mixers, hand-held,
    beating eggs with, 11, 17–18
English Cream
    Banana Macaroon, 92
    Blueberries and Bananas with, 26
    Brown Sugar, with Glazed Pecans,
        93
    Chocolate, with Banana Chips, 95
    Pecan Praline, 103

Figs
    (in) Chocolate Marquise Surprise,
        97
    Plumped, in Hot Buttered
        Mincemeat Sauce, 59
Filberts. See Hazelnuts
Filled Poppy-Seed Cake, 173
Flammes, 237, 280
Fleur-de-Lys, 277
Flour
    flouring cake pans, 15–16
    sifting and measuring, 16–17
    tossing berries with, 154
Food processors, note on, 13
    chopping nuts in, 12
    grinding citrus zest, 12
Freezing
    cake layers, 22
    custard, 77
    pies, 115
Frozen Chocolate Squares, 271
Frozen desserts, 251–81. See also
        Bombe; Coupes; Ice Creams
Fruit(s)
    baking, 51
    -based custards, 75, 83–88

desserts, 23–71
  as filling for cake-tarts, 225
  Mixed, in Cantaloupe Rings, 31
  poaching, 51, 56
  selecting fresh, 25
  Sour Cream, Pie, Coconut Crust, 131
  See also Individual fruits

Gelatin
  dissolving, 13–14
  in pies, setting time, 115
Gianduja, 65
Gingerbread, Nana's, 168
Glazed Nut Topping, Blueberry Compote with, 58
Glazing techniques, for nuts, 30, 66, 94–95
Grand Marnier
  Chocolate Syrup Bundt Cake with, 165
  flavoring whipped cream, 14
  Lemon Cream with White Raisins in, 99
  Meringue Trifle, 190
  Peaches with, Whipped Cream, 35
  Raspberry Coupe with, 269
  See also Liqueurs
Grapes(s)
  in Rum Butterscotch Cream, 28
  in Sherried Cream, 29
  (in) Sour Cream Fruit Pie, 131
  varieties of, 28
Grating citrus zest, 11–12
Ground Almond Cake, 149

Hand-held electric mixers, using, 11, 17–18
Hazelnut(s), Toasted, Coupe, 261

Ice cream(s)
  commercial, 254–55
  Fleur-de-Lys, 277
  Frozen Chocolate Squares, 271

Molds
  Chocolate Toasted-Almond Bombe, 274
  Strawberry-Banana, Ring, 279
  in trifles, 180
  See also Bombe; Coupes
Ice cubes, using to cool pie fillings, 115
Icing
  Chocolate Cream, for Chocolate Cream Cake, 209, 211
  Cream Cheese Brown Sugar, for Brown Sugar Pecan Squares, 157
Ingredients
  in ice cream, 254
  mixing, for cake, 148
  notes on selection, 7–8
  warming, 148
Inverted-bowl test, 11

Jelly,
  acidic, purpose of, 188
Jelly Roll Trifle, 188

Kiwi fruit
  Lizzy Burt's Strawberry-, Pavlova, 123
  Strawberries and, in Cointreau Frozen Cream, 45
Kuchen
  Blackberry, 153
  substituting other fruits for, 154

Ladyfingers, in trifle, 182, 186, 190, 194
Lemon(s)
  candied peel, preparing, 101–102, 264
  Coupe with Candied Peel, 263
  Cream, with White Raisins in Grand Marnier, 99
  curd, 263
  No-Bake, Cheesecake, 140
  zest, grating, 11–12

Light Carrot Almond Cake, 158
Lime(s)
  candied peel, preparing, 101–102
  Meringue Cake, 245
  Mousse with Candied Peel, 101
  Pineapple with Carrot-, Cream, 39
  zest, grating, 11–12
Liqueur(s)
  flavoring trifles with, 180
  Orange, Cake with Walnuts and
    Raisins, 169
  in whipped cream, 14, 56
  See also Amaretto; Cointreau;
    Grand Marnier
Lizzy Burt's Strawberry-Kiwi
  Pavlova, 123
Loaf, Chocolate Mousse, 214

Macadamia nuts, (in) Fleur-de-Lys,
  277
Macaroon
  Banana, English Cream, 92
  Crust, for Banana Cream Pie, 118
  Peach, Trifle, 192
Magic Deep-Dish Coconut Custard
  Pie, 122
Maple Pecan Coupe, 265
Marbleized Cranberry Sauce, 52
Margarine vs. butter, 8–9
Measuring techniques, for flour,
  16–17
Melon, (in) Mixed Fruit in
  Cantaloupe Rings, 31
Meringue
  Grand Marnier, Trifle, 190
  Lime, Cake, 245
  Lizzy Burt's Strawberry-Kiwi
    Pavlova, 123
  piping, 246
  shell, for fruit desserts, 123–25
  Walnut Pavlova with Peaches,
    126
Microwave oven, 13–14
  alternatives to, 13–14
Milk, warming, 148

Mincemeat
  Sauce, Plumped Figs in Hot
    Buttered, 59
  Turnovers, 135
Mini Strawberry Cookie Tarts, 136
Mixed Fruit in Cantaloupe Rings,
  31
Mixing bowls, size of, 17
Mixing ingredients, for cake, 148
Mocha, Almond Torte, 202
Molasses (cookie crust)
  Pecan, for No-Bake Pumpkin Pie,
    129
  for Raspberry Cheesecake, 142
Mousse
  Chocolate
    Cake with Strawberries, 212
    Loaf, 214
    Marquise Surprise, 97
  Lime, with Candied Peel, 101
  Tangerine, 105
  Two-Layered Raspberry, 107

Nana's Gingerbread, 168
No-Bake
  Lemon Cheesecake, 140
  Pumpkin Pie, Molasses Pecan
    Crust, 129
Nouvelle Pâtisserie, 225
Nuts(s)
  chopping, 12
  crusts, 120, 128
  glazing, 30, 66, 94–95
  Topping, Blueberry Compote with
    Glazed, 58
  See also Individual nuts

Old-Fashioned Bread Pudding, 80
Orange(s)
  Custard, 85
  Liqueur, Cake with Walnuts and
    Raisins, 169
  See also Cointreau; Grand
    Marnier; Liqueurs
  Sauce, Pears with Cranberry-, 37

(in) Sour Cream Fruit Pie, 131
zest, grating, 11–12
Oven
microwave, 13–14
opening door of while baking,
19–20

Pain de Gênes, 149
Parchment paper, lining cake pans
with, 15
Passion fruit, in meringue shell, 124
Pastry bag
piping
flammes, 237, 280
meringue, 246
whipped cream, 14–15
tips for, a selection, 14, 114, 137,
237, 260, 276, 278
Pavlova(s)
Lizzy Burt's Strawberry-Kiwi, 123
Walnut, with Peaches, 126
Peach(es)
Babcock, 36
with Blueberries in Raspberry
Cream, 34
with Grand Marnier Whipped
Cream, 35
Macaroon Trifle, 192
(in) Mixed Fruit in Cantaloupe
Rings, 31
Sliced
in Blackberry Sauce, 32
in Peach Sauce, 61
in Spiced Red Wine, 62
Walnut Pavlova with, 126
Walnut Torte with, and Cream, 219
Peanut(s)
Chopped, Crust, for Peanut Butter
Cream Pie, 128
Peanut Butter
Cream Pie, Chopped Peanut
Crust, 128
(in) Pear Surprise with Chocolate
Sauce, 65
Raisin Bread Pudding with, 81

Pear(s)
Chocolate, Betty, 63
Chocolate-Coated, Cake, 242
with Cranberry-Orange Sauce, 37
to poach, 68
with Raspberry Sauce, 66
and Raspberry Trifle, 194
selection of, note, 38
with Soft-Frozen Strawberry
Sauce, 38
in Spiced Red Wine Coupe, 266
Surprise with Chocolate Suace, 65
Pecan(s)
Apple, Cake, 152
Balls with Brown Sugar Sauce,
268
Brown Sugar, Squares, 155
Caramel, Surprise Cake, 240
to glaze, 94–95
Glazed, Brown Sugar English
Cream with, 93
Maple, Coupe, 265
Molasses, Crust, for No-Bake
Pumpkin Pie, 129
Pineapple, Upside-Down Cake,
171
Praline Cream, 103
Spiced, Torte with Bananas, 216
Pie(s)
Almond Cream, Almond Crust,
116
Ambrosia, 131
baking hints, 115–16
Banana Cream, Macaroon Crust,
118
Chocolate, Walnut Chocolate
Crust, 120
crust, unsticking, 115–16
decorating with whipped cream,
114–15
fillings, cooling with ice cubes,
115
freezing, 115
Magic Deep-Dish Coconut
Custard, 122

No-Bake Pumpkin, Molasses
    Pecan Crust, 129
pan, oiling, 115
Peanut Butter Cream, Chopped
    Peanut Crust, 128
Sour Cream Fruit, Coconut Crust,
    131
Strawberry, Almond Shortbread
    Crust, 133
See also Cheesecakes; Crusts; Tarts;
    Turnovers
Pineapple
    Angel Food Trifle, 196
    Apricot-, Cheesecake, 138
    with Carrot-Lime Cream, 39
    with Coconut, Brown Sugar, and
        Rum, 41
    -Coconut Cake-Tart, 233
    Pecan Upside-Down Cake, 171
Piping techniques
    with chocolate icing, 211, 242
    onto cookie base, 136–37
    meringue rosettes, 246
    pie decorations, 114–15
    with whipped cream, 14–15
    See also Pastry bag
Plum(s)
    Crisp, 68
    Italian "prune," 68
    Purple, Chantilly, 42
    selecting ripe, 42
    types, 68
Plumped Figs in Hot Buttered
    Mincemeat Sauce, 59
Poaching techniques
    blueberries, 51
    cherries, 51, 56
    pears, 68
Poires Hélène. See Chocolate Pear
    Betty
Poppy-seed, Filled, Cake, 173
Praline
    Cream, Pecan, 103
    powder, to make, 103–104
Preparation time, categories of, 3–6

Pudding
    Old-Fashioned Bread, 80
    Raisin Bread, with Peanut Butter,
        81
Puff-pastry sheets, in turnovers,
    135
Pumpkin Pie, No-Bake, Molasses
    Pecan Crust, 129
Purple Plums Chantilly, 42

Queen of Sheba Chocolate Squares,
    162

Raisin(s)
    Bread Pudding with Peanut
        Butter, 81
    Orange Liqueur Cake with
        Walnuts and, 169
    White, Lemon Cream with, in
        Grand Marnier, 99
Raspberry(ies)
    -Applesauce Cake-Tart, 235
    Cheesecake, 142
    Coupe with Grand Marnier, 269
    Cream, Peaches with Blueberries
        in, 34
    in kuchen, substituting for other
        fruit, 154
    in meringue shell, 124
    Pear and, Trifle, 194
    Sauce, Pears with, 66
    Strawberry-, Custard, 87
    Two-Layered, Mousse, 107
Refrigerating
    cake layers, 22
    custard, 77
Rhubarb
    Compote with Fresh Strawberries,
        70
    note on cooking, 70
Rum
    Butterscotch Cream, Grapes in, 28
    flavoring trifles, 180
    Pineapple with Coconut, Brown
        Sugar, and, 41

Sauce(s)
 Blackberry, Sliced Peaches in, 32
 Brown Sugar
  Pecan Balls with, 268
  Walnut, Baked Apples with, 53
 Chocolate
  Cake, 164
  cocoa–brown sugar–apple juice–butter, to serve on coupe, 259
  Pear Surprise with, 65
  Strawberries with Chocolate Cream and, 44
 Cranberry
  Marbleized, Baked Apples with, 52
  -Orange, Pears with, 37
 Mincemeat, Plumped Figs in Hot Buttered, 59
 Peach, Sliced Peaches in, 61
 Raspberry, Pears with, 66
 Strawberry, Pears with Soft-Frozen, 38
Shell
 Meringue, 123–25
 Tart, 226
Sherried Cream, Grapes in, 29
Shortbread, Almond, Crust, for Strawberry Pie, 133
Sifting flour, 16–17
Sliced Peaches
 in Blackberry Sauce, 32
 in Peach Sauce, 61
Sour Cream
 Fruit Pie, Coconut Crust, 131
 Strawberries in Strawberry, 46
Spiced
 Apple Brownie Trifle, 180
 Custard with Apples, 77
 Pecan Torte with Bananas, 216
 Red Wine
  Peaches in, 62
  Pears in, Coupe, 266
Spiderweb effect, 211

Spongecake(s)
 Baking techniques, 15–22
  beating egg yolks, 10
  testing for doneness, 19
  unmolding, 20–21
 as bases and shells for cake desserts, 225–26
 Basic Butter, Layers (base), 228
  Caramel Pecan Surprise Cake, 240
  Chocolate-Coated Pear Cake, 242
  Lime Meringue Cake, 245
 Butter Spongecake Tart Shell, 226
  See also Cake-Tarts
 Chocolate Butter (base), 230
  Strawberry Taj Mahal, 247
 splitting layers, 21–22
Springform pans
 buttering and flouring, 16
 unmolding, 21
Strawberry(ies)
 -Banana Ice-Cream Ring, 279
 Bavarian Cream Trifle with, 186
 with Chocolate Cream and Chocolate Sauce, 44
 Chocolate Mousse Cake with, 212
 hulling, 48
 and Kiwis in Cointreau Frozen Cream, 45
 Lizzy Burt's, -Kiwi Pavlova, 123
 in meringue shell, 124
 Mini, Cookie Tarts, 136
 Mixed Fruit in Cantaloupe Rings, 31
 Pie, Almond Shortbread Crust, 133
 -Raspberry Custard, 87
 Rhubarb Compote with, 70
 Sauce, Pears with Soft-Frozen, 38
 storing, note, 279
 in Strawberry Sour Cream, 46
 Taj Mahal, 247
Streusel, 154
Sugar
 author's comment, 8
 effect on egg yolk, 148

Tangerine
  Cake-Tart, 238
  Mousse, 105
Tart(s)
  Mini Strawberry Cookie, 136
  Shell, Butter Spongecake, 226
  Strawberry Pie, Almond
      Shortbread Crust, 133
  See also Cake-Tarts
Tips, choosing for pastry bag, 14,
      114, 137, 237, 260, 276, 278
Toasted Hazelnut Coupe, 261
Toothpick test, 19
Topping(s)
  Glazed Nut, Blueberry Compote
      with, 58
  See also Cream; English Cream;
      Sauces; Whipped Cream
Torte(s)
  Almond Mocha, 202
  Spiced Pecan, with Bananas, 216
  Walnut, with Peaches and Cream,
      219
Trifle(s), 177–97
  Bavarian Cream, with
      Strawberries, 186
  Blueberry, 182
  cake for, 179
  Chocolate Truffle, 184
  flavoring with orange liqueur, 180
  Grand Marnier Meringue, 190
  ice cream in, 180
  ingredients in, 179–80
  Jelly Roll, 188
  origin of, 179
  Peach Macaroon, 192
  Pear and Raspberry, 194
  Pineapple Angel Food, 196
  serving, 180
  Spiced Apple Brownie, 180
Truffle
  Chocolate
    made from extra chocolate
        coating, 244
    Trifle, 184

Turnovers, Mincemeat, 135
Two-Layered Raspberry Mousse,
      107

Upside-Down Cake, Pineapple
      Pecan, 171

Walnut(s)
  Blueberry Compote with Glazed
      Nut Topping, 58
  Chocolate Crust, for Chocolate
      Pie, 120
  Orange Liqueur Cake with, and
      Raisins, 169
  Pavlova with Peaches, 126
  Sauce, Brown Sugar, Baked
      Apples with, 53
  Torte with Peaches and Cream,
      219
Water bath, baking custards in,
      76
Whipped Cream
  Creme Chantilly, 42
  for decorations, 14
  flammes, 237, 280
  flavoring with liqueurs, 14, 56
  Grand Marnier, Peaches with,
      35
  piping, 14–15
    on cookie tart, 136–37
    over a coupe, 260
    on pies, 114–15
Whisk, number of wires in, 173
Wiggle test, 76–77
Wine, Spiced Red
  Peaches in, 62
  Pears in, Coupe, 266
World's Best Black Cherry Compote,
      56

Zabaglione, an eggless, 29
Zest, citrus
  grating, 11–12
  grinding in food processor,
      12